How to Protect Your Children from Child Abuse:
A Parent's Guide

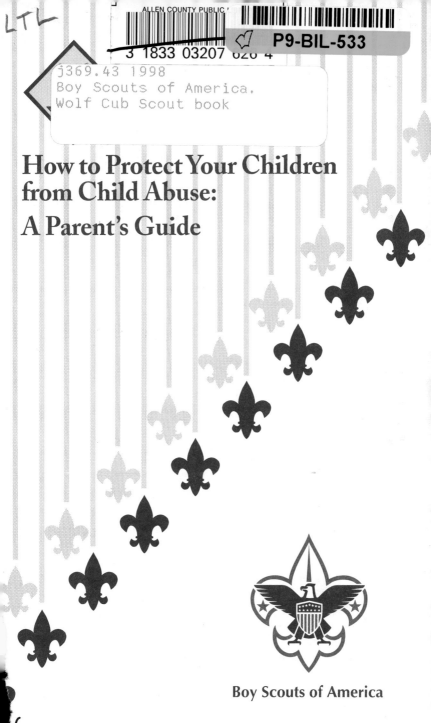

Boy Scouts of America

Introduction·

Our children are often faced with choices affecting their development and safety. As parents, we can do our best to provide education and guidance to prepare our children to make the best decisions. One way that we do this is to talk with our children. Some subjects are easy to discuss with our children—sports, their grades in school, their friends, and many other features of our daily lives. Other things are more difficult for us to discuss, including child abuse—especially child sexual abuse.

Although discussing child abuse with your children may be difficult for you, it is very important. Perhaps the most important step parents can take to protect their children from abuse is to have open communication in the home. Research has shown that children whose parents talk to them about preventing abuse are more effective at fending off assaults. Your role is very important.

More than three million reports of child abuse are received each year, including half a million reports of *child sexual abuse.* As a major youth-serving organization, the Boy Scouts of America has a unique opportunity to help protect the youth of our nation. This booklet is designed to give you essential information that should help you teach your children how to protect themselves.

If your son is a new Cub Scout, this might be the first time that you have seen this *Parent's Guide.* For parents who have other sons in Scouting, and for those whose sons have advanced in Cub Scouting, we hope that you are familiar with this guide and have discussed its contents with your children. In either case, we encourage you to make this information part of a continuing family effort that reinforces the concepts included in this guidebook.

We do not expect that your son will become a victim of child abuse. It is extremely important, however, that if he ever faces an abusive situation, he knows that there are adults in his life who will listen and respond in a supportive manner. The purpose of this booklet is to help you and your son establish, or reinforce, open communication on this sensitive topic.

Section I.
Information for Parents

Using This Booklet

This booklet is divided into two sections. The first section is for your information. It contains information about child abuse and provides some tips to help parents talk about child abuse with their Cub Scout–age sons. The second section is for you to share with your son. **It begins with a few simple exercises for you both to complete together as part of his requirements for the Bobcat badge**. The second section also contains some optional activities for him.

It is important that you read the entire booklet before you and your son do any of the exercises together. Once you are comfortable with the topics in this booklet, you will be able to present the information in ways he can understand. Feel free to reword an exercise in order to help your child gain a better understanding.

Child Abuse:
Basic Information for Parents

An abused or neglected child is a child who is harmed, or threatened with physical or mental harm, by the acts or lack of action of a person responsible for the child's care. There are several forms of abuse: physical abuse, emotional abuse, and sexual abuse. Child neglect is a form of abuse that occurs when a person responsible for the care of a child is able, but fails, to provide necessary food, clothing, shelter, or care. Each state has its own definitions and laws concerning child abuse and child neglect.

Child abuse and neglect are serious problems for our society. The number of cases reported has increased each year since 1976, when statistics were first kept. A brief discussion of each form of abuse follows:

Neglect

A child is neglected if the persons he depends on do not provide food, clothing, shelter, medical care, education, and supervision. When these basic needs are *deliberately withheld,* not because the parents or caregivers are poor, it is considered neglect. Often parents or caregivers of neglected children are so overwhelmed by their own needs that they cannot recognize the needs of their children.

Physical Abuse

Physical abuse is the deliberate injury of a child by a person responsible for the child's care. Physical abuse often stems from unreasonable punishment, or of punishment that is too harsh for the child. Sometimes, physical abuse occurs when caregivers react to stress. Drinking and drug abuse by caretakers have become more common contributing factors in physical abuse cases.

Physical abuse injuries can include bruises, broken bones, burns, and abrasions. Children experience minor injuries as a normal part of childhood, usually in places such as the shins, knees, and elbows. When the injuries are found in soft-tissue areas on the abdomen or back, or don't seem to be typical childhood injuries, it is possible that the child has been physically abused.

Emotional Abuse

Emotional abuse is harder to recognize, but is just as harmful to the child than other forms of abuse. Emotional abuse damages the child's self-esteem and, in extreme cases, can cause developmental problems and speech disorders. A child suffers from emotional abuse when constantly ridiculed, rejected, blamed, or compared unfavorably with brothers, sisters, or other children.

Expecting too much from the child in academics, athletics, or other achievements is a common cause of emotional abuse by parents or other adults. When a child can't meet these expectations, he feels that he is never quite good enough.

Sexual Abuse

When an adult or an older child uses his or her authority over a child to involve the child in sexual activity, it is child sexual abuse, and that person is a child molester. The molester might use tricks, bribes, pressure, threats, or force to persuade the child to join in sexual activity. Sexual abuse includes any activity performed for the sexual satisfaction of the molester, including acts ranging from exposing one's sex organs (exhibitionism), observing another's sex organs or sexual activity (voyeurism), to fondling and rape.

Here are a few facts you should know about child sexual abuse:

- Child sexual abuse occurs to as many as 25 percent of girls and 14 percent of boys before they reach 18 years of age.

- Boys and girls could be sexually abused at any age; however, most sexual abuse occurs between the ages of 7 and 13.

- Eighty to 90 percent of sexually abused boys are molested by acquaintances who are nonfamily members.

- Females perform 20 percent of the sexual abuse of boys under age 14 (prepubescents).

- Children are most likely to be molested by someone they know and trust.

- Few sexually abused children tell anyone that they have been abused. Children are usually told to keep the abuse secret. This could involve threats, bribes, or physical force.

- Children might feel responsible for their abuse and fear an angry reaction from their parents.

Sexual Molestation by Peers

Approximately one-third of sexual molestation is committed by other children. If your child tells you about club initiations in which sexual activity is included, or if your child tells you about inappropriate or tricked, pressured, or forced sexual activity by other children, this is a form of sexual abuse and you need to take steps to stop the activity. This kind of sexual misconduct is serious and should not be ignored.

Children who molest other children need professional help. They are much more likely to respond to treatment when young than are adults who began in adolescence to molest children and received no treatment, and continued to do so into adulthood.

Parents and others who work with children need to distinguish between normal sexual behavior of children and abusive behavior. All children are curious about sexual behavior as a part of growing up. This behavior is not appropriate when it is forced, when the person who provokes the activity has more power, or when the sexual behavior lacks consent. When parents are concerned about their son's sexual behavior, they should try to talk with him and discuss what worries them specifically about his behavior.

Signs of Sexual Abuse

The clearest sign that a child has been sexually abused is his statement saying that he was. Children often do not tell about their abuse, however, so parents should be alert for other signs. These are some signs to watch for:

- *Hints, indirect messages*—Refusing to go to a friend's or relative's home for no apparent reason; for example, "I just don't like him anymore."

- *Seductive or provocative behavior*—Acting out adult sexual behavior or using sexual language a young child is unlikely to know.

- *Physical symptoms*—Irritation of genital or anal areas.

The following are common signs that children are upset and need parental support. They might also be signs that your child is being sexually abused:

- *Self-destructive behavior*—Using alcohol or drugs, deliberately harming himself, running away, attempting suicide, or sexual recklessness or promiscuity.

- *Unhappiness*—Undue anxiety and crying, sleep disturbances, or loss of appetite.

- *Regression*—Behaving like a younger child, thumb sucking, or bed-wetting.

6

- *Difficulty at school*—Sudden drop in grades, behavioral problems, or truancy.

The presence of any of these signs should not be taken as an absolute sign of sexual abuse, but, if present for longer than several days, should be a sign that your child needs your help for whatever is bothering him.

Preventing Child Abuse

Except for sexual abuse of boys, the great majority of child abuse happens within families. Preventing sexual abuse outside of the family requires a different approach than preventing abuse that involves parents. Prevention efforts for emotional and physical abuse as well as neglect generally focus on helping the abusers, often the parents, change their behavior.

Some physical and emotional abuse stems from reactions by parents to the stresses in their lives. By learning to recognize these stresses, and then taking a time-out when the pressures mount, we can avoid abusing those we love. The next page lists some alternatives to physical and emotional abuse for overstressed parents. These suggestions come from the National Committee to Prevent Child Abuse.

Alternatives to Child Abuse

The next time everyday pressures build up to the point where you feel like lashing out—**Stop!** Try any of these simple alternatives. You'll feel better . . . and so will your child:

- Take a deep breath. And another. Then remember you are the adult.

- Close your eyes and imagine you're hearing what your child is about to hear.

- Press your lips together and count to ten; or, better yet, to twenty.

- Put your child in a time-out chair. (Remember this rule: One time-out minute for each year of age.)

- Put yourself in a time-out chair. Think about why you are angry: Is it your child, or is your child simply a convenient target for your anger?

- Phone a friend.

- If someone can watch the children, go outside and take a walk.

- Splash cold water on your face.

- Hug a pillow.

- Turn on some music. Maybe even sing along.

- Pick up a pencil and write down as many *helpful* words as you can think of. Save the list.

Few parents mean to abuse their children. When parents take time out to get control of themselves before they grab hold of their children, everybody wins.

In addition to these alternatives, parents and other child caregivers may want to think about the following questions* suggested by Douglas Besharov, the first director of the U.S. National Center on Child Abuse and Neglect, regarding the ways they discipline their children.

- Is the purpose of the punishment to educate the child or to vent the parent's anger?

- Is the child capable of understanding the relationship between his behavior and the punishment?

- Is the punishment appropriate and within the bounds of acceptable discipline?

- Is a less severe, but equally effective, punishment available?

- Is the punishment degrading, brutal, or extended beyond the limits of the child's endurance?

- If physical force is used, is it done carefully to avoid injury?

These questions help to define the boundaries between acceptable discipline and child abuse. Other causes of child abuse inside the family might be much more complex and require professional help to resolve.

Preventing sexual abuse outside the family calls for a different approach. Because parents cannot guarantee a safe environment for their children outside the home, preventing sexual abuse focuses on training the youth—the potential target of the abuse—about the "three Rs" of Youth Protection: *recognizing* schemes and situations used by child molesters; *resisting* attempts of molesters; and *reporting* anyone who tries to molest.

*Adapted from Douglas J. Besharov. *Recognizing Child Abuse: A Guide for the Concerned.* New York: Free Press, 1990.

Talking with Your Child About Sexual Abuse

It is very difficult for many parents to talk to their children about sexual abuse. The information in this section, and the exercises in the youth section, are intended to make that task easier.

The following points should help you and your child talk about sexual abuse prevention:

• *If you feel uncomfortable discussing sexual abuse with your child, let him know.* When you feel uncomfortable discussing sexual abuse with your children and try to hide your uneasiness, your children might misinterpret the anxiety and be less likely to approach you when they need help. You can use a simple statement like, "I wish we did not have to talk about this. I am uncomfortable because I don't like to think that this could happen to you. I want you to know that it's important, and you can come to me whenever you have a question or if anybody ever tries to hurt you."

• *Select words your child understands.* One main concern of parents is finding words to explain sexual abuse. Most experts on child abuse prevention believe that children should learn the proper names for their genitalia; however, if you are uncomfortable with using the names of body parts, use whatever terms your child understands.

• *Provide the opportunity for your child to practice Youth Protection skills.* Learning is more effective when children can practice the skills they are taught. Practicing the exercise of their rights (see Section II. Information for Children) with parents gives children confidence.

Many parents feel that teaching children about sexual abuse will take away their children's innocence. Many children are at risk of sexual abuse because they do not have the maturity to understand why a child molester would want to look at, touch, or otherwise violate them. This, in part, explains why children who are sexually abused at a young age do not realize that they were abused until they are older. It also explains a child's confusion if the parents or other adults overreact when the child tells about sexual abuse.

When a Child Discloses Abuse

If your child becomes a victim of abuse, your first reaction can be very important in helping him through the ordeal. The following guidelines may help you:

- **Don't** panic or overreact to the information your child tells you.

- **Don't** criticize your child or tell your child he misunderstood what happened.

- **Do** respect your child's privacy and take your child to a place where the two of you can talk without interruptions or distractions.

- **Do** reassure your child that he is not to blame for what happened. Tell him that you appreciate being told about the incident and will help to make sure that it won't happen again.

- **Do** encourage your child to tell the proper authorities what happened, but try to avoid repeated interviews that can be stressful for the child.

- **Do** consult your health care provider or other child abuse authority about the need for medical care or counseling for your child.

> You should show real concern, but NOT alarm or anger, when questioning your child about possible child abuse.

Finally, if your child has been sexually abused, do not blame yourself or your child. People who victimize children are not easy to identify. They come from all walks of life and all socioeconomic levels. Often they have positions of status—they go to church, hold regular jobs, and are active in the community. Child molesters are sometimes very skilled at controlling and using children, often by giving them excessive attention, gifts, and money. Child molesters use their skills on parents and other adults, disguising their abusive behavior behind friendship and care for the child.

Resources

BSA Youth Protection Materials

Along with this booklet, the Boy Scouts of America has an educational video for use by Cub Scout packs or dens. This award-winning production provides age-appropriate information about sexual abuse of boys.

It Happened to Me is a video for Cub Scout–age boys that shows common situations in which sexual abuse could occur. The video discusses how child molesters often resort to tricks for gaining access to their victims. It emphasizes that if a boy has been sexually abused, he should talk to his parents or other trusted adults. The video also stresses that it is not the child's fault if he has been sexually abused. It is the child molester who is responsible.

> *It Happened to Me* should be shown to boys 6 to 10 years of age *only* when a parent or other adult responsible for the child's care is present with the child.

This videotape is available from your BSA local council. The BSA encourages Cub Scout packs or dens to view the video annually. A meeting guide supporting the video's use can be found in the *Cub Scout Leader Book* (1994 and later editions). Copies may also be obtained from your council.

For Scouting's leaders and parents, the BSA has a video-taped training session, *Youth Protection Guidelines: Training for Volunteer Leaders and Parents,* available from your BSA local council with regular training sessions scheduled in most districts. The training addresses many questions that Scout volunteers and parents have regarding child sexual abuse.

In addition to these videotaped materials, the BSA some-times provides Youth Protection information to its members and families through *Boys' Life* and *Scouting* magazines.

Other Sources of Child Abuse Prevention Information

National Center for Child Abuse and Neglect
U.S. Department of Health and Human Services
P.O. Box 1182
Washington, DC 20013
800-394-3366

National Committee to Prevent Child Abuse
332 South Michigan Avenue, Suite 1600
Chicago, IL 60604-4537
312-663-3520

National Center for Missing and Exploited Children
2101 Wilson Boulevard, Suite 550
Arlington, VA 22201
800-843-5678

Section II.
Information for Children

The *Child's Bill of Rights* outlines some specific ways your child can protect himself. You should discuss these and the Basic Rules of Safety for Children with your child before completing the Bobcat Youth Protection requirements. These could provide the information that your son needs to help him respond to the situations in the exercises.

Child's Bill of Rights

When feeling threatened, you have the right to

- Trust your instincts or feelings.

- Expect privacy.

- Say no to unwanted touching or affection.

- Say no to an adult's inappropriate demands and requests.

- Withhold information that could jeopardize your safety.

- Refuse gifts.

- Be rude or unhelpful if the situation warrants.

- Run, scream, and make a scene.

- Physically fight off unwanted advances.

- Ask for help.

You should remind your son that these are actions that will give him the power to protect himself, and that some of these might not be appropriate for situations where he is not threatened.

14

Basic Rules of Safety for Children

Cub Scout–age children benefit from having concrete safety *rules*. It is important, however, to stress that traditional cautions about "strangers" are not enough to protect our children. Children have different ideas than adults do about who a stranger might be. In addition, the person who harms a child is usually someone the child knows. It might be more helpful to teach your children to recognize possibly threatening situations or actions.

Discuss the following safety rules with your child:

- If you are in a public place and get separated from your parent (or the person in charge of you), do not wander around looking for him or her. Go to a police officer, a checkout counter, the security office, or the lost-and-found area and quickly tell someone in charge that you have been separated from your parent and need help.

- You should not get into a car or go anywhere without your parent's permission.

- Adults and older youths who are not in your family and who need help (such as finding an address or locating a lost pet) should not ask children for help; they should ask other adults.

- You should use the buddy system and try not to go anyplace alone.

- Always ask your parent's permission before going into someone else's home.

- No one should ask you to keep a special secret when someone has been scared or hurt by the secret. If this happens, tell your parent or teacher.

- If someone insists on taking your picture or videotaping you and taking your clothes off, tell your parent or teacher.

- No one should touch you in ways or places that make you feel bad. You should not touch anyone else in ways that will make them feel bad. You should ask an adult you trust questions whenever you are mixed up about someone's touch or behavior.

- You have the right to say "No!" to anyone who tries to take you somewhere, touches you, or makes you feel uncomfortable in any way.

These are some simple safety rules that can be approached in the same nonfrightening manner in which you tell your child not to play with fire. They emphasize situations common to many child molestation cases.

Personal Protection Rules for Computer On-line Services

When you're on-line, you are in a public place, among thousands of people who are on-line at the same time. Be safe by following these personal protection rules and you will have fun:

- Keep on-line chats with strangers to public places, not in e-mail.

- Do not tell anyone on-line your real last name, phone numbers at home or school, your parents' workplaces, or the name or location of your school or home address unless you have your parent's permission first. Never give your password to anyone but a parent or other adult in your family.

- If someone shows you e-mail with sayings that make you feel uncomfortable, trust your feelings. You are probably right to be watchful. Do not answer. Tell a parent what happened.

- If somebody tells you to keep what's going on between the two of you secret, tell a parent.

- Be careful whom you talk to. Anyone who starts talking about subjects that make you feel uncomfortable is probably an adult posing as a kid.

- Pay attention if someone tells you things that don't fit together. One time an on-line friend will say he or she is 12, and another time will say he or she is 14. That is a warning that this person is lying and may be an adult posing as a kid.

- Unless you talk to a parent about it first, never talk to any-body by phone if you know that person only on-line. If someone asks you to call—even if it's collect or a toll-free, 800 number—that's a warning. That person can get your phone number this way, either from a phone bill or from caller ID.

- Never agree to meet someone you have met only on-line any place off-line, in the real world.

- Watch out if someone on-line starts talking about *hacking,* or breaking onto other people's or companies' computer systems; *phreaking* (the "ph"sounds like an "f"), the illegal use of long-distance services or cellular phones; or *viruses,* on-line programs that destroy or damage data when other people download these onto their computers.

- Promise your parent or an adult family member and your-self that you will honor any rules about how much time you are allowed to spend on-line and what you do and where you go while you are on-line.

Bobcat Requirements

1. Child Abuse and Being a Good Cub Scout

When a boy joins the Cub Scouting program, he assumes a duty to be faithful to the rules of Scouting as represented in the Cub Scout Promise, Law of the Pack, and Cub Scout motto. The rules of Scouting don't require a Scout to put himself in possibly dangerous situations—quite the opposite, we want Cub Scouts to "be prepared" and to "do their best" to avoid these situations.

We hope that you will discuss these rules with your Cub Scout and be sure that he understands that he should not risk his safety to follow the rules of Cub Scouting.

Cub Scouting's Principles

The Cub Scout Promise includes the phrase, "To help other people." This means that a Cub Scout should be willing to do things for others that would please them, but only when his parent has given permission and knows where he is and who he is with.

The Law of the Pack includes the phrase, "The Cub Scout follows Akela." Akela is a good leader and should never ask you to do something that you feel bad about. If Akela, who might be a teacher, coach, or other youth leader, ever asks you to do something you think is bad, as a Cub Scout you have the right to say "No!" and tell your parents or another adult you trust.

2. What If . . .

In this activity the parent describes situations that the child should recognize as possibly dangerous. Once the parent describes a situation, the child tells or shows what he would do if ever faced with a similar situation. After each situation, some possible responses are listed.

For some of these situations you might already have set rules. You should not change your rules in response to the exercise unless there is new information that you have not previously considered. You should also feel free to reword the situation if that helps your child understand the situation better.

Situations and Suggested Actions for Each

What if you are home alone, the telephone rings, and a voice on the other end asks if your parents are home? What would you do?

- Tell the caller your parents are busy and cannot come to the phone.

- Take a message and the phone number of the caller.

- If the message needs an immediate response, call your parent.

- Do not tell the caller you are home alone.

- Let the answering machine answer and do not pick up the phone until you are sure who the caller is.

What if an adult invites you on a camping trip and suggests that you allow him to take your picture when you are not wearing clothes? What would you do?

- Tell that person you do not want to have your picture taken when you do not have your clothes on.

- When you return home, tell your parents what happened.

- Be very careful around that person in the future, and be sure to tell your parents anything that bothers you about that person.

What if a neighbor comes to you and says that your parent is sick and you must go with him or her? This neighbor is not a person you have been told it's okay to go with. What would you do?

• If you are at school, ask the principal or your teacher to help you make sure your parent really sent this person for you.

• If you are at home or somewhere else, call the emergency number your parents gave you, such as where they work, or a close relative, for help in making sure your parent sent this person.

• Do not go anywhere without checking with the person you have been told to contact in this kind of situation.

What if you are in a public rest room and someone tries to touch you in ways or places that make you feel uncomfortable? What would you do?

• Yell "STOP THAT" as loudly as you can.

• Run out of the room as quickly as possible.

• Tell your parent, a police officer, security guard, or other adult (such as your teacher) what happened.

What if you are walking to school in the rain and a car stops and the driver asks if you want a ride? What would you do?

• Stay away from the car. You do not need to get close to the car to answer.

• Unless you have your parent's permission to ride with the person, say "No, thank you." If the driver keeps asking, say "No!," then get away.

• Tell your teacher when you get to school and tell your parent when you get home.

What if you are playing on the playground and an adult comes up to you and asks you to help find his or her lost puppy? What would you do?

- If you do not know the person, stay away and tell a teacher or other adult you trust.

- Adults should ask other adults for help. Before you help that person, you must get your parent's permission.

- Tell your parent what happened.

What if you are walking down the street and an elderly neighbor tells you that you'll get a quarter to help carry groceries? The person asks you to come into his or her house. What would you do?

- Get permission first.

- Do not ever go into anyone else's house without your parent's permission.

- Tell your parent about the person.

What if an older child you know invites you to play a game, and to pretend that he or she is the doctor and you are the patient? This child tells you to take off all of your clothes so that the "doctor" can examine the "patient." What would you do?

- Keep your clothes on.

- If he or she persists, say "No!," then yell and get away.

- Tell your parent.

BOBCAT

Other Youth Protection Activities (Not Part of the Bobcat Requirements)

My Safety Notebook

This exercise will help your child avoid situations that could lead to abuse or molestation. The safety notebook can be a loose-leaf notebook or pages stapled together for which your child has made an original cover. (Elective 9: Art, Bear Cub Scout requirements; Artist activity badge, Webelos Scout requirements.)

This safety notebook gives your child a place to list emergency telephone numbers, including parents' work numbers and a neighbor or friend's number to call when parents are unavailable. (Achievement 4: Know Your Home and Community, Wolf Cub Scout requirements.) In addition, your child can list the safety rules that you and he have discussed together. Encourage your child to decorate each page with pictures and drawings that illustrate some of the rules.

He may also want to list other kinds of safety guidelines, such as rules for bicycle safety. (Achievement 9: Be Safe at Home and on the Street, Wolf Cub Scout requirements. Achievement 14: Ride Right, Bear Cub Scout requirements; Readyman activity badge, Webelos Scout requirements.)

"My Safety Notebook" is intended to be a fun activity for getting across some serious concerns. It is a personalized reference that can reassure your child that he knows how to respond when confronted by a potentially dangerous situation.

Plays and Skits

Sometimes children enjoy creating a script for a play or skit that will dramatize their understanding of the safety rules. The skit could then be presented to other children as a service project. (Showman activity badge, Webelos Scout requirements; Elective 2: Be an Actor, Wolf Cub Scout requirements.) As a parent, you can guide the creation of the script so that the situations reflect an understanding of the rules and give an opportunity for practicing the skills. Children need to feel that they can protect themselves.

As pointed out earlier, children learn Youth Protection strategies better and are able to apply them when necessary if they practice these skills.

Family Meeting

A child must feel comfortable telling his parent about any sensitive problems or experiences in which someone approached him in an improper manner, or in a way that made him feel uncomfortable. Studies have shown that more than half of all child abuse incidents are never reported because the victims are too afraid or too confused to report their experiences.

Your children need to be allowed to talk freely about their likes and dislikes, their friends, and their true feelings. You can create open communication through family meetings where safety issues can be talked about by the entire family. (Family Member activity badge, Webelos Scout requirements.) Some of the activities suggested here could be done in the setting of a family meeting.

No. 46-014
Boy Scouts of America
1998 Printing

Wolf
Cub Scout Book

Welcome to the Wolf Cub Scout Book!

I am Akela. I will be your leader and friend. I will guide you along the Wolf trail.

Contents

Illustrations of Akela by Robert Depew

33106
ISBN 0-8395-3106-0
©1998 Boy Scouts of America
Revised 1998

10 9 8 7 6 5 4 3 2 1

Parent Guide

How to help your boy follow the Bobcat, Wolf, and Arrow Point trails

If you could give your boy the greatest gift of all, what would it be? It wouldn't be money or anything money can buy. Whether you are rich or poor, the greatest gift is within your power because that gift helps a boy become a person with a good feeling about himself and a genuine concern for others. Cub Scouting can help you provide this gift.

Your Son, Scouting, and You

As a parent, you want your boy to grow up to be self-reliant and dependable—a person of worth, a caring individual. Scouting has these same goals in mind for him.

Since 1910 we've been weaving lifetime values into fun and educational activities designed to help parents teach their sons how to make good decisions throughout their lives and give them confidence as they become the adult leaders of tomorrow.

In a society where your son is often taught that winning is everything, Cub Scouting teaches him to *do his best* and *be helpful to others* as expressed in the Cub Scout Promise, motto, and Law of the Pack.

A Cub Scout den will involve your boy in a group of boys his own age where he can earn status and recognition. There he will also gain a sense of personal achievement from the new skills he learns.

The Purposes of Cub Scouting

Cub Scouting is the phase of the program offered by the Boy Scouts of America for boys in first through fifth grade (or 7-, 8-, 9-, and 10-year-old boys). The purposes of Cub Scouting are to help parents and community organizations serve boys by

- Positively influencing character development and encouraging spiritual growth

- Helping boys develop habits and attitudes of good citizenship

- Encouraging good sportsmanship and pride in growing strong in mind and body

- Improving understanding within the family

- Strengthening their ability to get along with other boys and to respect other people

- Fostering a sense of personal achievement by helping boys develop new interests and skills

- Showing how to be helpful and do one's best

- Providing fun and exciting new things to do

- Preparing boys to become Boy Scouts

Cub Scouting

Your Cub Scout is a member of a den. Most dens have six to eight boys and meet once a week. Den meetings are a time for learning new things and having fun. Dens are led by a team of adult volunteers—the den leader and assistant den leader(s). Den leaders are usually parents of boys in the den. Your Cub Scout is also a member of a pack. Most packs have several dens and meet once a month. Pack meetings usually follow a suggested theme and are a time for boys to be recognized for their accomplishments during the month, to perform skits and songs they've learned in den meetings, and to have fun with the entire family.

Packs are led by a Cubmaster and pack committee. Like the den leaders, the Cubmaster and assistants are volunteers and are usually parents of boys in the pack. Most pack committees consist of parents and members of the pack's chartered organization. The pack committee makes plans for pack meetings and activities and takes care of the "business" items necessary for a quality pack program.

The pack is owned by a community organization that is granted a charter by the Boy Scouts of America to use the Scouting program. This chartered organization might be a school, service club, religious group, or other group interested in youth. The chartered organization approves the leadership of the pack, provides a meeting place, and operates the pack within the guidelines and policies of the organization and the Boy Scouts of America.

Akela's OK

As you look through this book, you'll see places for "Akela's OK." That usually means your okay. Akela (ah-KAY-la) is the boy's leader. At home, that is you; at den meetings, it is the den leader; at school, it is the teacher. Almost all electives and achievements are done by you and your Cub Scout at home, not in the den meeting. This book is filled with more than two hundred pages of activities for you and your son to enjoy together. Once your Cub Scout has done his best, you can approve the completion of the requirement and the den leader will record his progress in the den records.

1 *Mary Keuning*   [date here]   *Karen Bass*
BOBCAT TRAIL   Akela's OK   Date   Recorded by den leader

Notes for Akela

Throughout the *Wolf Cub Scout Book,* special notes for you are printed along with the requirements for special projects that require the supervision and participation of adults. Watch for these "Notes for Akela." They are printed in a smaller type size for your easy identification.

The Bobcat Trail

The first rank that your boy will earn as a Cub Scout is Bobcat. You'll find his trail on pages 00 through 00. Along this trail are the Cub Scout Promise, the Law of the Pack, and the Cub Scout motto. These are the three most important things a boy must learn because they will help him through all of the trails of Scouting.

One part of the Bobcat trail is to read and complete the exercises in the booklet *How to Protect Your Children from Child Abuse.* Child abuse is a problem in our society, and this booklet will help you help your child to avoid potentially abusive situations.

When you and your boy have followed the eight tracks of the Bobcat, he may wear his Bobcat badge. It will be presented at the pack meeting.

The Wolf Trail

After your Cub Scout has earned his Bobcat badge, he can start along the Wolf trail. This is a big adventure for a boy, one the Boy Scouts of America hopes all boys will complete.

When you have okayed the tracks your boy has filled in for all twelve achievements, he may become a Wolf Cub Scout. How quickly your boy progresses is up to him and you. He should do his best to complete each track; that's a part of the promise he made to become a Bobcat and it is the Cub Scout motto—Do Your Best. Don't okay a track if you both know that he can do a better job. Move on to something else, then go back and try again.

The important thing is to keep him interested by working on the trail with him as often as possible.

Progress Toward Ranks

Your boy doesn't have to wait until he completes his entire Wolf trail before being recognized for his work. When he completes any three achievements, his den leader can present the Progress Toward Ranks emblem to him. It's a diamond with a plastic thong, and is worn on the button of the right pocket of his uniform shirt. Each time he completes three achievements he will receive another gold bead. After he gets his fourth gold bead, he will be ready to receive his Wolf badge at a pack meeting.

The Arrow Point Trail

Your Cub Scout can also search the Arrow Point trail. On the Wolf trail, the main sections were called achievements, things that we would like all boys to do. On the Arrow Point trail, the main sections are called electives, choices that a boy can make on his own and with your guidance.

To earn a Gold Arrow Point to wear beneath his Wolf badge, a boy must complete any ten elective projects of the more than one hundred choices shown in the book. For every ten additional electives he completes, the Wolf Cub Scout qualifies for a Silver Arrow Point to wear beneath the Gold. He can earn as many Silver Arrow Points as he wants until he completes the second grade (or turns 9). Arrow Points are presented at the pack meeting after he receives his Wolf badge.

Your boy should begin earning achievements toward his Wolf badge as soon as he completes the Bobcat requirements. Completing electives for Arrow Points generally should wait until after he has earned his Wolf badge, and he cannot receive Arrow Points until he has been awarded his Wolf badge. He might, however, find some electives that he could be completing before he earns the Wolf badge. Some of the activities in "Sports," Wolf Elective 20, might be examples. As long as he completes these electives after he has earned his Bobcat, you may credit him for them, but be sure to keep him focused on the twelve achievements until he completes them.

1 *Mary Denning*   [date here]   *Karen Bass*
ARROW POINT TRAIL   Akela's OK   Date   Recorded by den leader

Do Your Best

When has a boy completed an elective or achievement? When he, in your opinion as Akela, has completed the skill to the best of his ability. In Cub Scouting, boys are judged against their own standard, not against other boys.

If your Cub Scout has a mental or physical disability that prevents him from attempting an achievement, talk to your Cubmaster about using an elective as an alternative.

Baden-Powell, the founder of Scouting, based Cub Scouting on one of the stories in Rudyard Kipling's *Jungle Book.* It was called "Mowgli's Brothers." We know it as "The Story of Akela and Mowgli." Read the story twice, once to yourself and the second time to your Cub Scout.

The Story of Akela and Mowgli

Once upon a time in the jungles of India on a warm summer evening, Father Wolf awoke, stretched his paws, and prepared to go hunting.

The moon shone into the mouth of the cave where Mother Wolf lay sleeping with their four young cubs. Suddenly, a shadow crossed the opening of the cave and a whining voice said, "Good hunting, o' chief of the wolves, and good luck to your children." It was Tabaqui, the sneaky little jackal who, because he is too lazy to hunt for himself, picks up scraps left by other animals.

Father Wolf told him, "There is no food here, but come in if you wish."

Tabaqui said, "For a poor animal like myself a dry bone is a feast," and in no time at all he was cracking away on a bone at the back of the cave. Now Tabaqui was always ready to make trouble and to talk about others. He said, "Shere Khan, the mighty tiger, has changed his hunting ground. He hunts in these hills for the next moon." (Shere Khan was the tiger who lived about twenty miles away, near the big river.)

Father Wolf said, "By the Law of the Jungle, he has no right to change his hunting ground. He will scare the animals away for miles around."

Tabaqui said, "I could have saved myself the trouble of telling you. You can hear him now in the jungle below." And he trotted off to find the tiger.

Father and Mother Wolf listened. From the valley below, they could hear the angry whine of a tiger who had caught nothing and didn't care if the whole jungle knew it.

"The fool," said Father Wolf, "to start a night's hunting with all that noise!" The whine changed to a humming-purr, which is the noise a tiger makes when he is hunting man. Father Wolf said, "Are there not enough frogs and beetles that he must hunt man?"

Just then there was a most untigerish howl from Shere Khan, and Mother Wolf said, "He missed! What happened?"

Father Wolf ran out a few paces and looked down to a clearing where there were several woodcutters' huts. He said, "Shere Khan has had no more sense than to jump at the woodcutters' fire. He burned his feet! Tabaqui is with him and they have frightened all the people away."

"Listen," Mother Wolf said, "something is coming up the hill. Get ready!"

Father Wolf crouched and sprang, but as he sprang, he stopped himself in midair because what he saw was a little baby boy!

"Man!" he said. "A man-cub. Look!"

"I have never seen one," Mother Wolf said. "Bring him to me."

Father Wolf brought him into the cave and put him down beside Mother Wolf. The baby snuggled close to the young wolf cubs. "How little he is," said Mother Wolf.

Suddenly, the moonlight was blocked from the door of the cave by the great head and shoulders of Shere Khan.

"What does Shere Khan want?" said Father Wolf with angry eyes.

"The man-cub!" said Shere Khan. "Give him to me!"

Father Wolf said, "The wolves take orders only from Akela, the head of the wolf pack. The man-cub is ours."

The tiger's roar filled the cave with thunder. "The man-cub is mine. Give him to me!" said Shere Khan.

Mother Wolf sprang up quickly and said, "The man-cub is ours. You have frightened his family away. He shall not be killed. He shall live to run with the pack and hunt with the pack."

Shere Khan knew he could not fight the two wolves in the cave; therefore, he went away growling, snarling, and saying, "We will see what the pack has to say about this man-cub."

When the tiger had gone, Father Wolf said, "Shere Khan is right. What will the pack say?" But Mother Wolf had decided to keep him. And they called him Mowgli ("the frog") because his skin was smooth and without hair. Mowgli stayed with the young cubs.

When they were old enough to run, Father and Mother Wolf set off with them one night, through the jungle to a meeting of the wolf pack at the Council Rock. The Law of the Jungle states that wolves must gather to look over the new wolf cubs of the pack, so that they will know them and take care of them when they see them in the jungle.

As each young wolf was pushed into the circle, Akela, the great leader of the wolf pack, sitting high on the Council Rock, called, "Look at each cub, o' wolves. Look well." At last it was Mowgli's turn and Mother Wolf pushed him into the circle where he sat playing with some stones in the moonlight. Akela did not even twitch an ear as he called, "Look well, o' wolves."

From outside the circle came a roar from Shere Khan. "The man-cub is mine. Give him to me." Some of the wolves took up the cry,

"What do we want with a man-cub in the pack?"

There is a law that says if there is an argument as to the right of a cub to join the pack, two members must speak for him. Akela asked, "Who speaks for this cub?"

At first there was no answer, but then Baloo, the sleepy brown bear who teaches the cubs the Law of the Pack, stepped into the circle and said, "I will speak for the man-cub. Let him join the pack and I, myself, will teach him the law and the ways of the jungle."

"We need another," said Akela. "Who besides Baloo speaks?"

An inky black shadow dropped silently into the circle. It was Bagheera, the black panther, the mighty hunter who teaches the cubs the skills of the jungle. In his soft silky voice he said, "If there is a question about the right of a cub to join the pack, his life may be bought at a price. Isn't that the law?"

"Yes," said the pack.

"Then to Baloo's good word, I will add fresh meat which is in the valley below, if you will accept Mowgli into the pack."

The wolves cried, "Let him join. What harm can a man-cub do?" They looked him over; then, one by one, the wolves went down the hill, leaving Mowgli with Father and Mother Wolf, Baloo, and Bagheera at the Council Rock with Akela. Akela said, "Now take him away and teach him the Law of the Pack."

And that is how Mowgli joined the Seeonee Wolf Pack.

After you have read this Parent Guide, you may act as Akela. Indicate your willingness to serve by signing below.

I/We will be Akela in this *Wolf Cub Scout Book:*

Signature _____ Date _____

Signature _____ Date _____

Signature _____ Date _____

Signature _____ Date _____

Welcome to Cub Scouting!

You have heard how Mowgli met Akela (say ah-KAY-la). Just as that story says, in a real wolf pack all the wolves look to Akela, the leader, for guidance—when to work, when to learn, when to play.

Akela makes sure each young wolf in the pack gets the chance to learn about the world, and how to get along with other members of the pack.

There are times when Akela romps and plays games with members of the pack. But there are times when Akela, with a movement of his head or a steady gaze, commands the young wolves' attention.

Akela, the wolf pack leader, is caring and wise. He is both a friend and a teacher.

Like your parents, your teachers, and other adults who help you learn, Akela is your guide.

Throughout the pages of this book, Akela will guide you to your place in the pack. Along the Wolf trail, you will learn the Cub Scout Promise and the Law of the Pack.

You will learn new skills. You will try new things. Akela, your guide, will help you begin your exciting trail through Cub Scouting, and onward to Webelos Scouting.

Come! Be a part of the pack. Follow the trail.

We begin our trail by following Akela's friend, the Bobcat. Follow his trail first to become a Bobcat Cub Scout and to earn your place in the pack.

Bobcat Trail

Welcome to Our Pack!

Say hi to my friend the Bobcat. He has eight things for you to do.

HE SAYS

"Follow my Bobcat Trail."

When you have filled in all eight tracks, you can wear my badge.

Fill in this track when you have completed all eight tracks. You may also mark the Trail Summary on page 222.

I, ... ,
promise to do my best
To do my duty to God and
my country,
To help other people, and
To obey the Law of the Pack.

When you say you will do something,
that is a promise.

Duty to God means:
Put God first. Do what you know God
wants you to do.

And my country means:
Do what you can for your country.
Be proud that you are an American.

To help other people means:
Do things for others that would help them.

Obey the Law of the Pack means:
Be a good Cub Scout. Be proud that you
are one.

When you can say the
Promise, fill in my track.

1 _____   _____
Akela's OK   Date   Recorded by the den leader

Say the Law of the Pack. Tell what it means.

BOBCAT TRAIL

The Law of the Pack

The Cub Scout follows Akela.
The Cub Scout helps the pack go.
The pack helps the Cub Scout grow.
The Cub Scout gives goodwill.

The Cub Scout follows Akela (say Ah-KAY-la).

Akela is a good leader.
Your mother or father is Akela.
In the pack, your Cubmaster is Akela.
Your den leader is Akela.
At school, your teacher is Akela.

The Cub Scout helps the pack go.

Come to all the meetings. Do what you can to help. Think of others in the pack.

The pack helps the Cub Scout grow.

You can have fun when you are a part of the pack. Learn things from others. Do things with them.

The Cub Scout gives goodwill.

Smile. Be happy. Do things that make others happy. They don't have to be big things. Little things help, too.

When you can say the Law of the Pack and tell what it means, fill in my track.

Akela's OK   Date   Recorded by the den leader

Webelos

BOBCAT TRAIL

Webelos (say WE-buh-lows) is a Cub Scout secret. Cub Scouts know the secret. It is We'll Be Loyal Scouts.

We'll
Be
Loyal
Scouts
} **WeBeLoS**

Being loyal means that you will keep the Cub Scout Promise.

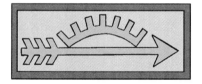

The Webelos Arrow of Light points the right way to go every day of the week. That is why the sun has seven rays—one for each day.

When you know what Webelos means, fill in my track.

| Akela's OK | Date | Recorded by the den leader |

4 Show the Cub Scout sign.
Tell what it means.

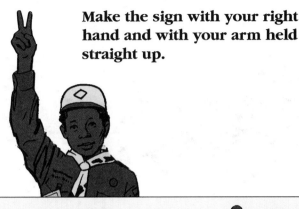

Make the sign with your right hand and with your arm held straight up.

Cub Scout Sign

The two fingers stand for two parts of the Promise—"to help other people" and "to obey." They look like a wolf's ears ready to listen to Akela.

Give the Cub Scout sign when you say the Cub Scout Promise or the Law of the Pack.

When you can give the sign and tell what it means, fill in my track.

Akela's OK	Date	Recorded by the den leader

5 Show the Cub Scout handshake.
Tell what it means.

BOBCAT TRAIL

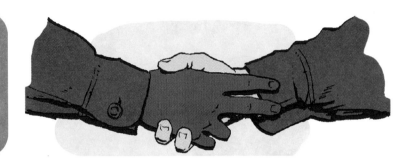

Cub Scout Handshake

Here's how to shake hands with another Cub Scout. Hold out your right hand just as you always do to shake hands. Put your first two fingers along the inside of the other boy's wrist.

This means that you help and that you obey the Law of the Pack.

When you can shake hands as a Cub Scout, fill in my track.

5 Akela's OK _____ Date _____ Recorded by the den leader

6

Say the Cub Scout motto.
A motto is a rule.

BOBCAT TRAIL

Cub Scout Motto

DO YOUR BEST is the Cub Scout motto.

It means

When you play a game, do your best to help your team.

When you study in school, do your best to learn from your teacher.

When you help at home, do your best to help your family. Whatever you do, do your best.

> When you know the motto and can tell what it means, fill in my track.

6

_____   _____
Akela's OK   Date   Recorded by the den leader

Bobcat Trail

25

7 Give the Cub Scout salute.
Tell what it means.

BOBCAT TRAIL

Cub Scout Salute

Salute with your right hand. Hold your fingers as you do for the Cub Scout sign. Keep the two straight fingers close together. Touch the tips of those fingers to your cap. If you are not wearing a cap, touch your right eyebrow.

A salute is a way to show respect. We salute the flag to show respect to our country.

When you can give the Cub Scout salute and tell what it means, fill in my track.

7 _____   _____
Akela's OK   Date   Recorded by the den leader

8 With your parent or guardian, complete the exercises in the booklet *How to Protect Your Children from Child Abuse.*

Child Protection Exercises

When you have completed these exercises with your parent or guardian, fill in my track.

8

Akela's OK

Date   Recorded by the den leader

Your Den

Your den is a group of boys who live in your general neighborhood. You might know and play with most of them.

About once a week you will meet with your den. Your den leader, the adult in charge of the meetings, will be Akela.

Your den leader will help guide you through the exciting Wolf trail that is part of the Cub Scout adventure. You will have fun doing that and other things.

You and other boys in your den will have fun getting ready for the pack meeting in many of your den meetings.

Cub Scouting is fun, and much of that fun starts in your den.

The den meeting is usually held in somebody's home. It might be held in your home.

What do you do at a den meeting? Lots of things. You'd better be on time or you will miss something.

When you get there, Cub Scouts might be playing a game or doing a puzzle.

When all the Cub Scouts are there, it is time to start the meeting.

You might salute the flag or say the Cub Scout Promise.

Maybe you will play a game that has something to do with the month's show idea; we call it a theme. Or you could do a stunt or skit or make something.

Before the meeting ends, you might be a part of the Living Circle ceremony. Hold out your left hand—palm down and thumb out. Hold the thumb of the boy on your left.

DO	SAY
Raise the Living Circle.	AH
Lower it.	KAY
Raise it.	LA
Lower it.	WE'LL
Raise it.	DO
Lower it.	OUR
Raise it.	BEST

Or you might end the meeting with this Cub Scout closing in sign language.

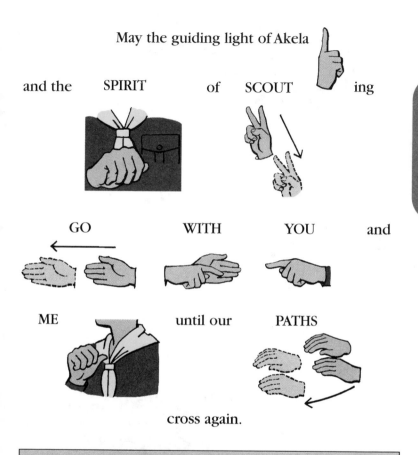

May the guiding light of Akela

and the   SPIRIT   of   SCOUT   ing

GO   WITH   YOU   and

ME   until our   PATHS

cross again.

Before you leave the den meeting, do three things:

1. Help clean up the room.
2. Be sure you have all your things.
3. Thank Akela (your leader).

Go home and get ready for more fun.

BOBCAT TRAIL

Your Pack

Wolves from many dens run in packs. The pack is one big happy family.

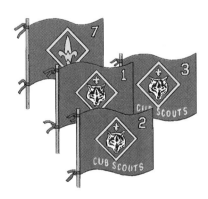

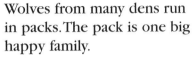

Your den belongs to a pack. You will meet members of other dens at a pack meeting.

A pack meeting is a show and each show has a new idea, such as Cub Scout fair, or blue and gold. Each den takes a part in the show.

But pack meetings are not just for Cub Scouts. Pack meetings are for families. They watch while you and other Cub Scouts do your stuff and get your badges.

Your pack might belong to a church or a school or something like that. Your pack meets there.

The pack leader is called a Cubmaster. The Cubmaster
is Akela for the pack.

Your Uniform

The Blue and Gold

The blue in your uniform is for truth. Gold is for sunlight, good cheer, and happiness. When you wear the Cub Scout uniform, people will know you are trying to be good and helpful.

Earn It

Uniforms cost money. You can help pay for yours. There are jobs that you can do at home or near where you live. Tell your folks you want to help. Everybody should have a job to do, and you should want to do your share.

Buy It

You cannot buy your uniform in just any store. Ask your leader where to buy it. Only Cub Scouts can buy a Cub Scout uniform.

Wear It

Wear your uniform to den and pack meetings. Wear it whenever you take part in something Cub Scouts do. Keep your uniform clean and neat. Hang it in a closet or fold it and put it in a drawer or on a shelf.

Now, follow my
Wolf Trail

My track is different from the Bobcat's. Cats don't show their claws, but wolves and dogs do.

Bobcat

Wolf

Fill in my tracks as you follow my trail. Not all the tracks have to be filled in. Sometimes you can choose. You may also fill in the tracks on the Trail Summary on pages 223 and 224.

1 Feats of Skill

You are growing. You are getting stronger. Try these feats of skill. Test your speed. Test your balance. Test your strength.

REQUIREMENT

1a

Play catch with someone ten steps away. Play until you can throw and catch.

a   Akela's OK   Date   Recorded by the den leader

REQUIREMENT

1b

Walk a line back and forth. Do it sideways, too. Then walk the edge of a board six steps each way.

NOTE for Akela: If a physician certifies that a Cub Scout's physical condition for an indeterminable time won't permit him to do three of these requirements, the Cubmaster and pack committee may authorize substitution of any three Arrow Point electives.

b   Akela's OK   Date   Recorded by the den leader

Feats of Skill

REQUIREMENT 1c

Do a front roll.

Akela's OK   Date   Recorded by the den leader

REQUIREMENT 1d

Do a back roll.

Akela's OK   Date   Recorded by the den leader

REQUIREMENT 1e

Do a falling forward roll.

Akela's OK   Date   Recorded by the den leader

Do ONE of the following (f, g, h, i, j, or k):
DO THIS

REQUIREMENT 1f

See how high you can jump.

Count down from ten to zero and coil your body for a blast-off.

When you come to zero, yell "Blast-off!" and jump as high into the air as you can. Land on your feet.

f   Akela's OK   Date   Recorded by the den leader

WOLF TRAIL

OR THIS

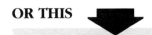 **REQUIREMENT 1g** Do the elephant walk, frog leap, and crab walk.

Elephant walk ⟶

WOLF TRAIL

Frog leap ⟶

Crab walk ⟶

g   _____   Date   Recorded by the den leader

Akela's OK

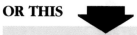

OR THIS

REQUIREMENT **1h** **Swim as far as you can walk in fifteen steps.**

Do this in shallow water with a grown-up who swims well.

NOTE for Akela: Measure at the side of the pool, or along the shore of a pond or lake.

Akela's OK   Date   Recorded by the den leader

WOLF TRAIL

OR THIS

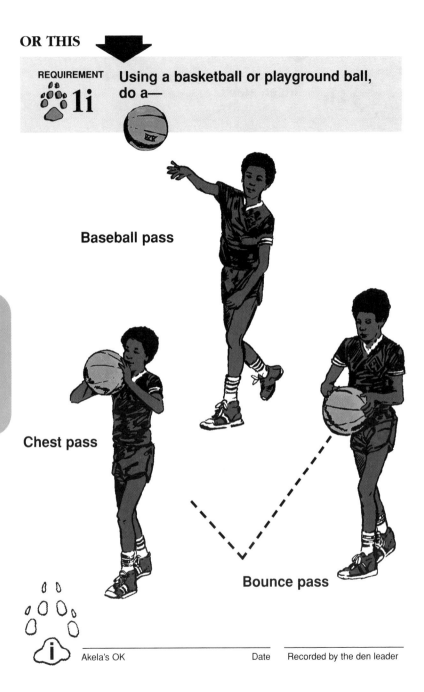

REQUIREMENT **1i**

Using a basketball or playground ball, do a—

Baseball pass

WOLF TRAIL

Chest pass

Bounce pass

_____ _____ _____
Akela's OK   Date   Recorded by the den leader

44

Wolf Trail • Achievement 1

OR THIS

REQUIREMENT **1j**   Do a frog stand.

j   Akela's OK   Date   Recorded by the den leader

OR THIS

REQUIREMENT **1k**   Run or jog for 10 minutes.
Or jog in place for 5 minutes.

k   Akela's OK   Date   Recorded by the den leader

Feats of Skill   45

2 Your Flag

Your flag stands for our country. Learn some ways to honor your flag.

Pledge of Allegiance

I pledge allegiance
to the flag of the
United States of America
and to the republic
for which it stands,
one nation under God,
indivisible, with liberty
and justice for all.

A **pledge** is a promise.
Allegiance is to be true.
Republic is our kind of government.
Nation is a country.
God is the one we worship.
Indivisible is one that cannot be
divided into pieces or parts.
Liberty is freedom for you and for others.
Justice is what is right and fair.

| Akela's OK | Date | Recorded by the den leader |

WOLF TRAIL

Lead a flag ceremony in your den.
Here are some ideas:

Get your den to stand in a straight line and face the flag. Salute and say the Pledge of Allegiance.

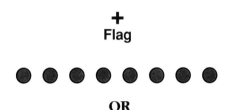

OR

Stand in a square formation. Bring in the flag. Salute and say the Cub Scout Promise.

OR

Stand in a circle around the flag. Salute and say the Pledge of Allegiance.

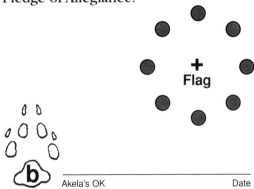

Akela's OK   Date   Recorded by the den leader

Tell how to respect and take care of the flag. Show three ways to display the flag.

Be careful **not** to

1. Let the flag get dirty.

2. Let the flag get torn.

3. Let the flag touch the ground.

Can you think of other ways to care for your flag?

Display the flag inside

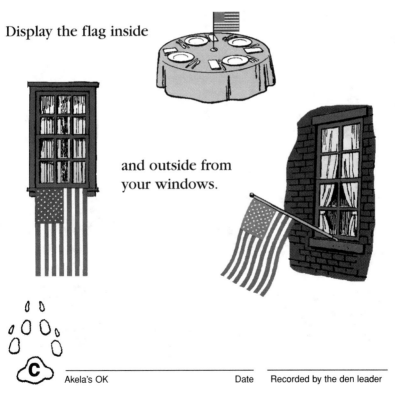

and outside from your windows.

WOLF TRAIL

_____   _____   _____
Akela's OK   Date   Recorded by the den leader

REQUIREMENT 2d Learn about the flag of your state or territory and how to display it.

WOLF TRAIL

ALABAMA

ALASKA

AMERICAN SAMOA

ARIZONA

ARKANSAS

CALIFORNIA

COLORADO

CONNECTICUT

DELAWARE

DISTRICT OF COLUMBIA

FLORIDA

GEORGIA

GUAM

HAWAII

IDAHO

ILLINOIS

INDIANA

IOWA

KANSAS

KENTUCKY

LOUISIANA

MAINE

MARYLAND

MASSACHUSETTS

MICHIGAN

MINNESOTA

MISSISSIPPI

MISSOURI

MONTANA

NEBRASKA

NEVADA

NEW HAMPSHIRE

NEW JERSEY

NEW MEXICO

NEW YORK

NORTH
CAROLINA

NORTH
DAKOTA

OHIO

OKLAHOMA

OREGON

PENNSYLVANIA

PUERTO RICO

RHODE
ISLAND

SOUTH
CAROLINA

SOUTH
DAKOTA

TENNESSEE

TEXAS

UTAH

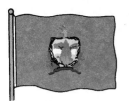
VERMONT

VIRGIN ISLANDS

VIRGINIA

WASHINGTON

WEST VIRGINIA

WISCONSIN

WYOMING

**Displaying the state flag
with U.S. flag and pack flag**

_____   _____
Akela's OK   Date   Recorded by the den leader

Your Flag   53

REQUIREMENT
2e

With the help of another person, fold the flag.

Salute as the flag is being lowered. After it is down, fold it and put it in a safe place.

Fold once.

Then fold again.

Fold corner
up and over.

Now fold down.

Keep folding
until it looks
like this.

Tuck
the end
in here. ▶

When the flag is folded correctly, it looks like the three-cornered hats worn during the American Revolutionary War and no red shows.

_____   _____   _____
Akela's OK   Date   Recorded by the den leader

Keep Your Body Healthy

Be healthy and strong. Learn what to do to be healthy.
Keep active to be strong.

REQUIREMENT 3a

Show that you know and follow the seven rules of health.

1. Take baths or showers often—once a day if you can. Use soap.

2. Wash your hands before meals and after using the toilet.

3. Brush your teeth before you go to bed and after breakfast. Brush your teeth or rinse your mouth after eating.

4. Drink lots of water (six to eight glasses a day).

5. Eat different kinds of food. Do most of your eating at mealtime. Stay away from too many sweets.

6. Run and play outdoors.

7. Get the sleep you need.

WOLF TRAIL

Akela's OK   Date   Recorded by the den leader

1. If you have a cold, stay away from other people.

2. Get lots of rest.

3. Turn your head away from others when you sneeze or cough. Cover your mouth and nose.

4. Wash your hands often, and always wash them after you sneeze.

WOLF TRAIL

| Akela's OK | Date | Recorded by the den leader |

Show what to do for a small cut on your finger.

1. Tell a grown-up about the cut.

2. Let the cut bleed a little.

3. Wash it with soap and
   water.

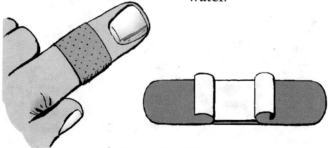

4. Cover it with a stick-on bandage.
   For a big cut, get help fast.

Akela's OK	Date	Recorded by the den leader

Keep Your Body Healthy

WOLF TRAIL

59

Know Your Home and Community

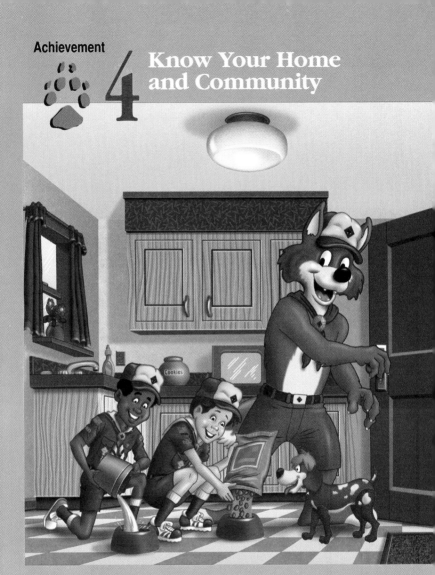

Sometimes your parents have to be somewhere else, and you must be home without an adult. If you can take care of yourself, no one will worry. You will be safe and happy. Here are some things to do when you are home alone, along with some other things to do to be responsible and helpful in your home.

REQUIREMENT 4a

Write down the phone numbers you need to have. Put them by your phone.

Police _____

Fire _____

Doctor _____

Mother at work _____

Father at work _____

Family friend _____

_____   _____
Akela's OK   Date   Recorded by the den leader

REQUIREMENT 4b

Tell what to do if someone comes to the door and wants to come in.

NOTE for Akela: Discuss with your boy what to do if someone wants to come in when your boy is home alone.

_____   _____
Akela's OK   Date   Recorded by the den leader

Know Your Home and Community

REQUIREMENT 4c

Tell what to do if someone calls on the phone.

NOTE for Akela: Discuss with your boy what to say if someone calls and your boy is home alone.

C

Akela's OK   Date   Recorded by the den leader

WOLF TRAIL

REQUIREMENT 4d

When I leave our home I will . . .

_____ Turn off the lights.

_____ Close and lock the windows.

_____ Turn off the water.

_____ Take care of pets.

_____ Have my key.

_____ Lock all of the doors.

NOTE for Akela: Help your boy to make sure everything is taken care of before he leaves the house.

d

Akela's OK   Date   Recorded by the den leader

REQUIREMENT 4e Talk with others in your home about helping. Agree on the home jobs you will do. Make a list of your jobs.

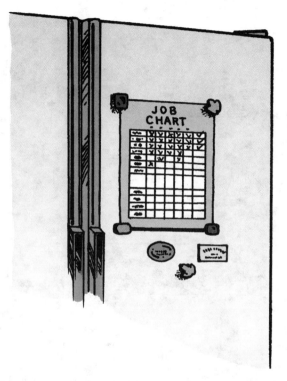

NOTE for Akela: You can teach your boy responsibility by helping him find jobs he can do to help around the home.

Akela's OK   Date   Recorded by the den leader

WOLF TRAIL

5 Tools for Fixing and Building

You can make something if you know how to use tools. You can fix things that are broken.

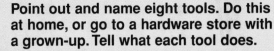

Plane to smooth wood

Hacksaw to cut metal

Handsaw for straight cuts in wood

File to smooth metal

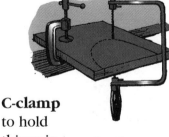

C-clamp to hold things in place

Coping saw for cutting curves in wood

Claw hammer to drive nails and pull them out

Plunger to open clogged drains

WOLF TRAIL

Awl to punch holes

Adjustable wrench to turn bolts or nuts.

Akela's OK   Date   Recorded by the den leader

REQUIREMENT 5b **Show how to use pliers.**

Slip-joint pliers

Slip the joint this way for small jobs.

Slip the joint this way for big jobs.

Akela's OK   Date   Recorded by the den leader

5c Use a screwdriver to drive a screw.

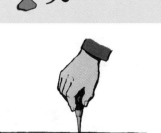

1. Start a hole in the wood with an awl or a nail.

2. A screw with soap on it is easier to turn.

3. Twist the screw into the hole.

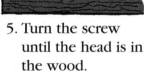

4. Pick the right screwdriver to fit the screw.

5. Turn the screw until the head is in the wood.

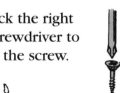

Akela's OK   Date   Recorded by the den leader

WOLF TRAIL

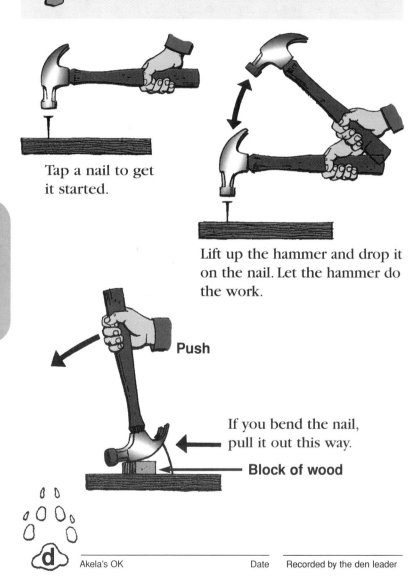

Tap a nail to get it started.

Lift up the hammer and drop it on the nail. Let the hammer do the work.

Push

If you bend the nail, pull it out this way.

Block of wood

d

Akela's OK   Date   Recorded by the den leader

Make a birdhouse, a set of bookends, or something else useful.

NOTE for Akela: Birdhouse kits and other projects are available at your local Scout shop.

_____   _____
Akela's OK   Date   Recorded by the den leader

Start a Collection

You can collect almost anything. Put your collection together so that you can show it to your family, den, and pack.

REQUIREMENT
6a

Make a collection of anything you like. Start with ten things. Put them together in a neat way.

Use an empty egg carton
for stones or things like that.

Hold shells in place
with wire or glue.

WOLF TRAIL

Use stamp hinges to put
stamps in a book or use
clear plastic holders.

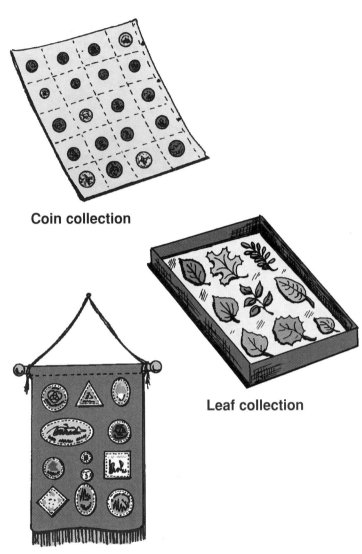

Coin collection

Leaf collection

Patch collection

6b **Show and explain your collection to another person.**

I showed and explained my collection to _____

_____

_____

b _____   _____
Akela's OK   Date   Recorded by the den leader

WOLF TRAIL

Our world is the only one we have. Take care of it. There are many ways you can help.

This achievement is also part of the World Conservation Award. (See page 216.)

REQUIREMENT 7a
Land, air, and water can get dirty. On a sheet of paper, list ways this can happen.

a Akela's OK Date Recorded by the den leader

REQUIREMENT 7b
It takes a lot of energy to make glass, cans, and paper products. You can help save energy by collecting these items for use again. Write the name of the recycling center closest to you. Find out what items you can save and send to this center.

Recycling bin

RECYCLING

 Akela's OK Date Recorded by the den leader

REQUIREMENT 7c With a grown-up, pick up litter in your neighborhood. Wear gloves to protect your hands against germs and cuts from sharp objects.

Akela's OK _____ Date _____ Recorded by the den leader

REQUIREMENT 7d With a grown-up, find three stories that tell how people are protecting our world. Read and discuss them together.

Akela's OK _____ Date _____ Recorded by the den leader

REQUIREMENT 7e

Besides recycling, there are other ways to save energy. List three ways you can save energy, and do them.

1. _____

_____

2. _____

_____

3. _____

_____

WOLF TRAIL

Keep the temperature in your home moderate—not too hot in the winter and not too cold in the summer.

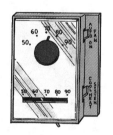

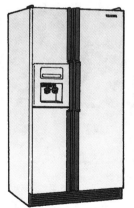

Keep the refrigerator door closed.

Akela's OK _____ Date _____ Recorded by the den leader

Your Living World   77

8 Cooking and Eating

It's fun to be the cook. The cook fixes the meal and might or might not use a stove. You won't need a stove for sandwiches and salads.

REQUIREMENT **8a** Study the Food Guide Pyramid. Name some foods from each of the food groups shown in the pyramid.

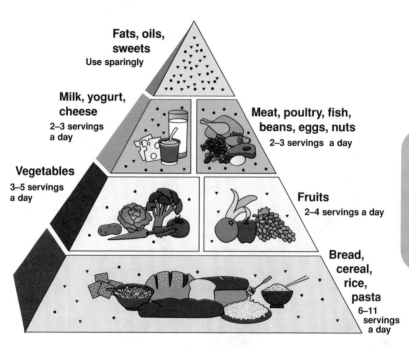

Fats, oils, sweets
Use sparingly

Milk, yogurt, cheese
2–3 servings a day

Meat, poultry, fish, beans, eggs, nuts
2–3 servings a day

Vegetables
3–5 servings a day

Fruits
2–4 servings a day

Bread, cereal, rice, pasta
6–11 servings a day

Food Guide Pyramid

WOLF TRAIL

Akela's OK   Date   Recorded by the den leader

REQUIREMENT 8b Plan the meals you and your family should have for one day. List things your family should have from the food groups shown in the Food Guide Pyramid. At each meal, you should have foods from at least three food groups.

Breakfast   Lunch   Dinner

_____   _____   _____

_____   _____   _____

_____   _____   _____

_____   _____   _____

b _____   _____
   Akela's OK   Date   Recorded by the den leader

REQUIREMENT 8c Help fix at least one meal for your family. Help set the table, cook the food, and wash the dishes.

Foods, dishes, knives, forks, and spoons must be clean. If they are dirty, you might get sick.

c _____   _____
   Akela's OK   Date   Recorded by the den leader

Wolf Trail • Achievement 8

REQUIREMENT 8d   **Fix your own breakfast. Wash and put away the dishes.**

d

Akela's OK   Date   Recorded by the den leader

REQUIREMENT 8e   **With a grown-up, help to plan, prepare, and cook an outdoor meal.**

WOLF TRAIL

e

Akela's OK   Date   Recorded by the den leader

Cooking and Eating

Be Safe at Home and on the Street

You can be careful and safe and still have fun. It's a lot more fun if you and other people don't get hurt. Let's learn how to be safe at home, and outside, too.

Keep tools and toys in their places.

Keep storage areas clear of waste and trash.

Use a step stool and stepladder to reach high places.

Be sure poisons are marked and stored where children can't get them.

Dry your hands before touching an electric switch.

Keep stairs clear. Help put things where they belong in closets, the attic, basement, or storeroom.

Keep closets neat.

Know where the water shutoff valve is.

Know where the electric fuse box or circuit breaker box is.

WOLF TRAIL

_____   _____
Akela's OK   Date   Recorded by the den leader

Be sure your home has at least one smoke detector. Check the battery.

Plan a family escape route from your home. Draw a floor plan and show the ways your family can get out in case of fire.

Ask a grown-up to keep gasoline and other dangerous things marked and away from fires or strong heat.

Keep matches where small children cannot reach them. **NEVER PLAY WITH MATCHES!**

Know where the fire exits are in all the buildings you enter. Look for EXIT signs.

Visit a fire station to learn how you can prevent fires.

Akela's OK | Date | Recorded by the den leader

Practice good rules of street and road safety.

Don't play in the street.

Walk on the left side of the road when there is no sidewalk. Face traffic, watch out for cars.

Obey traffic signs.

Cross at crosswalks. Watch traffic and look both ways before you step into the street.

Wear your seat belt while riding in a vehicle.

WOLF TRAIL

_____   _____   _____
Akela's OK   Date   Recorded by the den leader

REQUIREMENT **Know the rules of bike safety.**

Always wear a helmet.

Ride your bike in a safe place.

If you have to ride in the road, keep to the right.

Watch out for others.

Don't be a show-off.

Watch out for drain grates.

WOLF TRAIL

With your left arm, show others what you are going to do.

Right turn

Left turn

STOP

Stop or slow

Bicycle helmet

NOTE for Akela: Bikers should wear a Snell- or ANSI-approved bicycle helmet.

Akela's OK   Date   Recorded by the den leader

10 Family Fun

Here are some things to do that are fun for everyone.
There are games to play, places to go, and things to do
with your family.

Do TWO of these five requirements:

Make a game like one of these. Play it with your family.

Eagle Golf

Take turns dropping beans straight down into a small tin can. Each time a bean goes into the can is 1 point. To win, you must get as many points as you are old before the other players.

 ← Tin can

Beanbag Archery

The leader tosses a beanbag out as a target. The other players try to hit it. The closest one becomes the leader for the next toss.

Akela's OK	Date	Recorded by the den leader

REQUIREMENT 10b

Plan a walk. Go to a park or a wooded area, or visit a zoo or museum with your family.

b   _____   _____   _____

     Akela's OK   Date   Recorded by the den leader

REQUIREMENT 10c

Read a book or *Boys' Life* magazine with your family. Take turns reading aloud.

c   _____   _____   _____

     Akela's OK   Date   Recorded by the den leader

Decide with Akela what you will watch on television or listen to on the radio.

d Akela's OK

Date   Recorded by the den leader

Attend a concert, a play, or other live program with your family.

e Akela's OK

Date   Recorded by the den leader

11 Duty to God

A Cub Scout promises to do his duty to God. What is your duty to God? How do you do it? Your family can help you learn about God. This will help.

REQUIREMENT 11a Talk with your folks about what they believe is their duty to God.

Cub Scout Promise

I, ... ,
promise to do my best
To do my duty to God and
my country,
To help other people, and
To obey the Law of the Pack.

a   Akela's OK   Date   Recorded by the den leader

REQUIREMENT 11b Give some ideas on how you can practice or demonstrate your religious beliefs.

b   Akela's OK   Date   Recorded by the den leader

WOLF TRAIL

Duty to God

11c

Find out how you can help your church, synagogue, or religious fellowship.

I found out that _____

_____

_____

_____

_____

_____

WOLF TRAIL

C _____   _____   _____
   Akela's OK   Date   Recorded by the den leader

Religious Emblems Program

As a Cub Scout, you may earn the religious emblem of your faith. Talk to your religious leader about it.

Metta
Buddhist

Aleph
Jewish

Love for God
Meher Baba

Bismillah
Islamic

God and Me
Protestant

Unity of Mankind
Baha'i

Saint George
Eastern Orthodox

Saint Gregory
Armenian Churches

Joyful Servant
Churches of Christ

Love and Help
Unitarian Universalist

Love of God
Polish National Catholic

Parvuli Dei
Roman Catholic and Eastern-Rite Catholic

Dharma
Hindu

That of God
Religious Society of Friends (Quakers)

God and Country
First Church of Christ, Scientist

Religious emblems square knot

NOTE for Akela: Ask your religious leader or local council service center about the religious emblems programs available to Cub Scouts.

12 Making Choices

We have to make choices all the time. What to do. Where to go. Who to be with. Doing these requirements with your parent will help you learn how to make the best choices.

Do FOUR of these nine requirements:

REQUIREMENT **12a**
There is an older boy who hangs around Jason's school. He tries to give drugs to the children. What would you do if you were Jason?

I would _____

_____

_____

_____

a Akela's OK   Date   Recorded by the den leader

REQUIREMENT **12b**
Mel is home alone. The phone rings. When Mel answers, a stranger asks if Mel's mother is home. She is not. Mel is alone. What would you do if you were Mel?

I would _____

_____

_____

_____

b Akela's OK   Date   Recorded by the den leader

Making Choices   97

REQUIREMENT

12c

Justin is new to your school. He has braces on his legs and walks with a limp. Some of the kids at school tease him. They want you to tease him, too. What would you do?

I would _____

_____

_____

_____

Akela's OK   Date   Recorded by the den leader

REQUIREMENT

12d

Juan is on a walk with his little sister. A car stops and a man asks them to come over to the car. What would you do if you were Juan?

I would _____

_____

_____

_____

Akela's OK   Date   Recorded by the den leader

REQUIREMENT
12e

Matthew's grandmother gives him money to buy an ice-cream cone. On the way to the store, a bigger boy asks for money and threatens to hit Matthew if he does not give him some money. If you were Matthew, what would you do?

I would _____

_____

_____

_____

e   Akela's OK   Date   Recorded by the den leader

REQUIREMENT
12f

Chris and his little brother are home alone in the afternoon. A woman knocks on the door and says she wants to read the meter. She is not wearing a uniform. What would you do if you were Chris?

I would _____

_____

_____

_____

f   Akela's OK   Date   Recorded by the den leader

WOLF TRAIL

REQUIREMENT 12g

Sam is home alone. He looks out the window and sees a man trying to break into a neighbor's back door. What would you do if you were Sam?

I would _____

_____

_____

_____

g Akela's OK _____ Date Recorded by the den leader

REQUIREMENT 12h

Mr. Palmer is blind. He has a guide dog. One day as he is crossing the street, some kids whistle and call to the dog. They want you and your friends to call the dog, too. What would you do?

I would _____

_____

_____

_____

h Akela's OK _____ Date Recorded by the den leader

Some kids who go to Bob's school want him to steal candy and gum from a store, which they can share later. Bob knows this is wrong, but he wants to be popular with these kids. What would you do if you were Bob?

I would _____

_____

_____

_____

Akela's OK   Date   Recorded by the den leader

WOLF TRAIL

When you have filled in forty-nine of my tracks through all twelve parts of the Wolf trail, you have earned the right to wear my BADGE.

Your Wolf badge will be presented at the pack meeting.

You Are Now a

Wolf Cub Scout.

Arrow Point Trail

NOW, you can earn a
GOLD
Arrow Point
and
SILVER
Arrow Points.

This arrow point tells you
what to do.

Fill in this arrow point when
you have done it.

With your first ten filled-in
arrow points you can get your

GOLD
Arrow Point;

ten more gives you a

SILVER
Arrow Point;

and ten more gives you another

SILVER
Arrow Point;

and so on. You can keep track of your arrow points
on pages 225 and 226.

ARROW POINT
TRAIL

ELECTIVE 1

It's a Secret

Learn to send secret messages. Only those who know the secret code can read them. Learn to "talk" with your hands.

a Use a secret code.

You can use numbers for letters.

1	A	14	N
2	B	15	O
3	C	16	P
4	D	17	Q
5	E	18	R
6	F	19	S
7	G	20	T
8	H	21	U
9	I	22	V
10	J	23	W
11	K	24	X
12	L	25	Y
13	M	26	Z

ARROW POINT TRAIL

13	25	14	1	13	5	9	19	10	9	13	.
M	Y	N	A	M	E	I	S	J	I	M	.

23	8	1	20	9	19	25	15	21	18	19	?
W	H	A	T	I	S	Y	O	U	R	S	?

Or turn the alphabet upside down.

A	Z		N	M
B	Y		O	L
C	X		P	K
D	W		Q	J
E	V		R	I
F	U		S	H
G	T		T	G
H	S		U	F
I	R		V	E
J	Q		W	D
K	P		X	C
L	O		Y	B
M	N		Z	A

R ZN VRTSG
I AM EIGHT

SLD LOW ZIV BLF?

DSZG RH BLFI OZHG MZNV?

My code is _____

Akela's OK

Date   Recorded by the den leader

To make the ink, use  milk or

lemon juice.

Use a toothpick for a pen.

When the "ink" dries, you can't see it until you hold it over a light. The heat from the light will turn the "ink" light brown

ARROW POINT TRAIL

b
_____   _____ _____
Akela's OK   Date   Recorded by the den leader

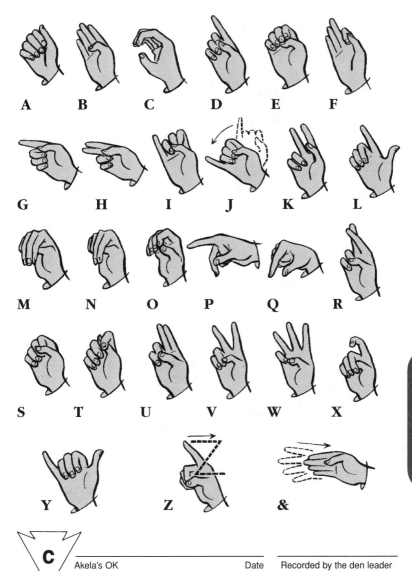

A   B   C   D   E   F

G   H   I   J   K   L

M   N   O   P   Q   R

S   T   U   V   W   X

Y   Z   &

C
Akela's OK   Date   Recorded by the den leader

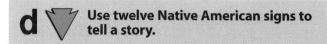
Sometimes, Native Americans would "talk" to others by using a sign language.

Native American Sign Language

Listen   I or Me   You or Him   Yes

Go   Come   Bring

Walk

Night

Sun

Moon

Hungry

Take

Run

With

Day

Eat

Drink

Sleep

Water

Friend

Talk

Man

Woman

Mind

Scout

Sunrise

Tongue

Heart

Good

Brave

True

What does this say?

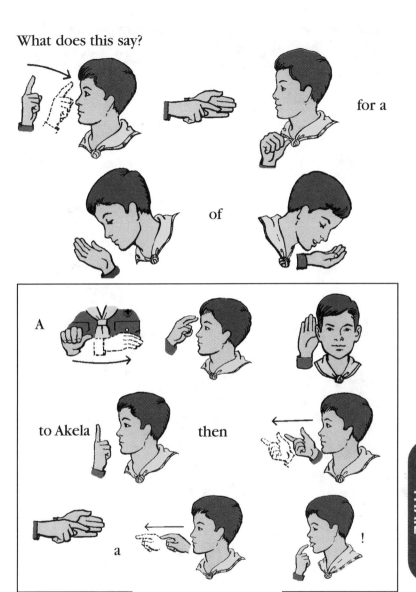

for a

of

A

to Akela

then

a

!

d

Akela's OK   Date   Recorded by the den leader

It's a Secret

111

Be an Actor

It's fun to be an actor. You can make-believe you are anyone you want to be.

a ▽ **Help to plan and put on a skit with costumes.**

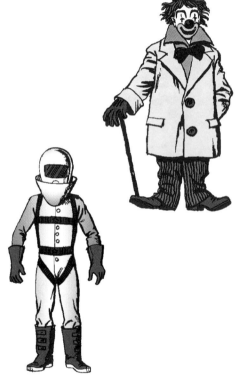

a
_____   _____
Akela's OK   Date   Recorded by the den leader

Make a tepee.

Cover the frame
with paper.

Make a pretend fire.

Tie rolled newspapers
and stack them.

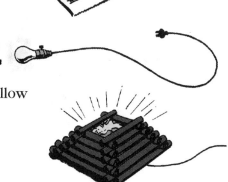

Insert a 15-watt yellow
or red bulb.

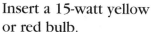

ARROW POINT TRAIL

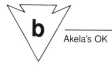

b / _____

Akela's OK   Date   Recorded by the den leader

1. Pound plastic bowls or coconut shells on a board for the clop-clop sound of horses.

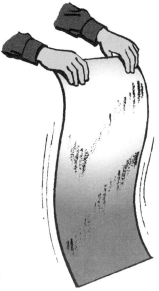

2. Rattle poster board or a metal sheet for thunder.

3. Roll dried peas in a can for rain.

4. Snap a belt or slap the floor or a table for a gunshot.

5. Use a bicycle bell for a telephone ring.

NOTE for Akela: Make these sounds behind a door or a screen so that the audience will think they are real.

Akela's OK   Date   Recorded by the den leader

Be an Actor

Akela's OK   Date   Recorded by the den leader

Akela's OK   Date   Recorded by the den leader

ELECTIVE

Make It Yourself

Watch carpenters and craftsmen at work. Learn how to handle tools; then pick a project and do it.

a Make something useful for your home or school. Start with a recipe card holder.

Recipe Card Holder

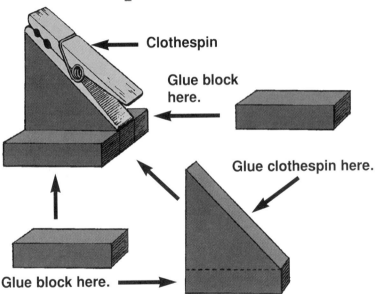

Clothespin

Glue block here.

Glue clothespin here.

Glue block here.

Sand the pieces smooth with sandpaper or steel wool before you put them together.

a

_____ _____ _____
Akela's OK   Date   Recorded by the den leader

AROW POINT TRAIL

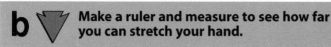

b Make a ruler and measure to see how far you can stretch your hand.

These spaces are centimeters. You can trace this on a piece of paper, cut it out, and then paste it on a piece of smooth wood to make a centimeter ruler.

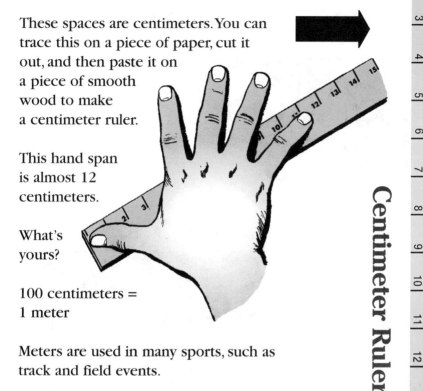

This hand span is almost 12 centimeters.

What's yours?

100 centimeters = 1 meter

Meters are used in many sports, such as track and field events.

Centimeter Ruler

0
1
2
3
4
5
6
7
8
9
10
11
12
13
14
15
16
17
18

b Akela's OK   Date   Recorded by the den leader

Bench Fork

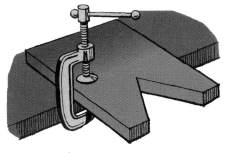

Clamp a piece of wood with a V cut in it to a workbench.

C-clamp

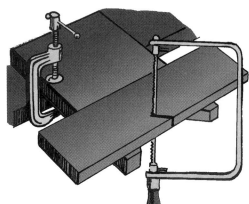

Hold another piece of wood on the fork and cut straight up and down with a coping saw. The fork lets you move the pieces around to cut curves.

Akela's OK	Date Recorded by the den leader

d Make a door stop.

Door Stop

Saw a wedge-shaped piece of wood from the end of a board. Sand it smooth. Paint or stain it.

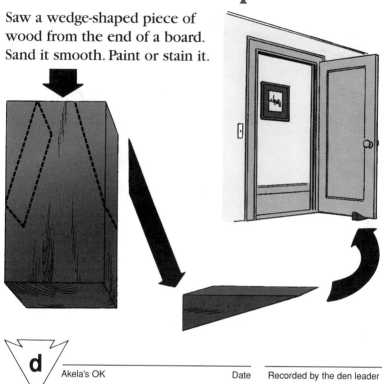

d

_____   _____
Akela's OK   Date   Recorded by the den leader

e Or make something else.

I made a _____

e

_____   _____
Akela's OK   Date   Recorded by the den leader

Play a Game

Play these games with children younger than you are, with other Cub Scouts, or with grown-ups.

a Play Pie-tin Washer Toss.

Each player tosses five washers at a pie tin. Score 1 point for each washer that stays in the pan.

a

| Akela's OK | | Date | Recorded by the den leader |

b 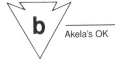 Play Marble Sharpshooter.

ARROW POINT TRAIL

Each player rolls five marbles at soda-bottle targets. Score 1 point for each marble that rolls between the bottles and misses them.

b

| Akela's OK | | Date | Recorded by the den leader |

Make five rings out of rope, rubber, wire, heavy cardboard, or folded newspaper.

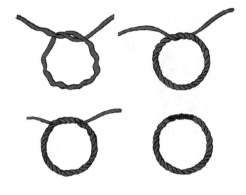

Toss the rings at a stick in the ground or on a stand.

Ringers = 3 points
Leaners = 1 point

ARROW POINT TRAIL

_____   _____
Akela's OK   Date   Recorded by the den leader

Play a Game   123

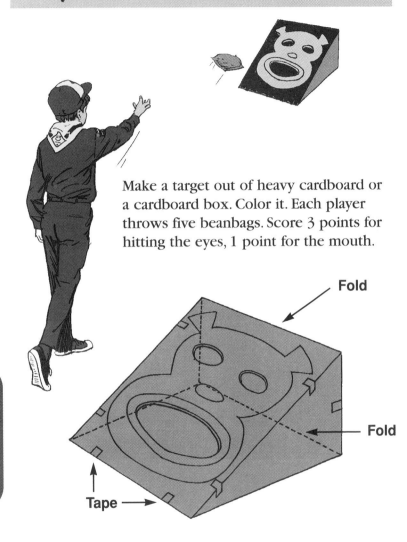

Make a target out of heavy cardboard or a cardboard box. Color it. Each player throws five beanbags. Score 3 points for hitting the eyes, 1 point for the mouth.

Fold

Fold

Tape →

d

Akela's OK _____ Date ___ Recorded by the den leader

Play a game of marbles.

Lag line

Put marbles inside
a circle like this.

Stand behind the
pitch line and toss
your shot toward
the lag line.

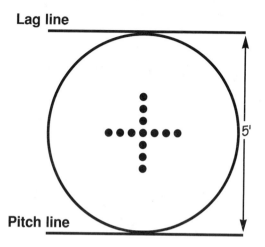

5'

Pitch line

The player nearest the lag line shoots first from the edge
of the circle.

The first player to knock seven marbles out of the circle
(with his shooter) is the winner.

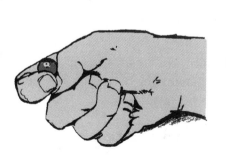

 Akela's OK   Date   Recorded by the den leader

Play a Game

ELECTIVE **Spare-Time Fun**

Ride the wind and waves with kites
and boats you can make yourself.

a **Explain safety rules for kite flying.**

 Fly kites away from electrical wires.

 Fly kites in fair weather. Put them away if a
storm approaches.

 Make kites with paper and wood, never
metal—it might attract lightning.

 Use dry string for kite line.

 Fly kites in an open field or park, never on a
street or railroad line.

 If a kite gets caught in wires, a treetop, or
somewhere else, have your parent or another
adult see if it can be saved.

Remember, have fun but play it safe.

ARROW POINT
TRAIL

a

_____   _____
Akela's OK   Date   Recorded by the den leader

Arrow Point Trail • Elective 5

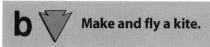
All you need for a
paper-bag kite is a big
paper bag and some
tape and string.

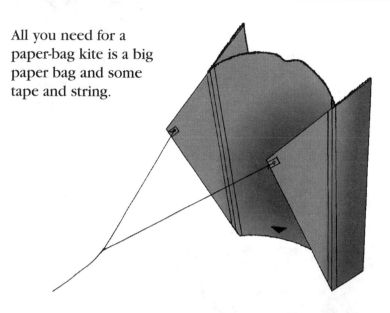

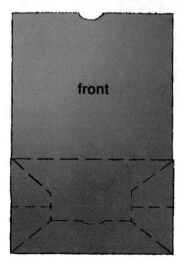

front

1. Cut out the bottom of the
   bag. Fold down the sides
   and make the bag flat.

ARROW POINT
TRAIL

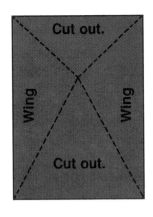

Cut out.

Wing

Wing

Cut out.

2. Turn the bag over. Make a mark in the center of the bag a third of the way down. Draw lines to the corners and cut out the pieces on this side.

Folded side

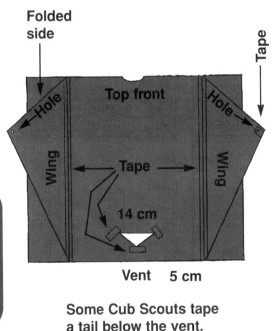

Tape

Hole

Top front

Hole

Wing

Tape

Wing

14 cm

Vent   5 cm

Some Cub Scouts tape a tail below the vent.

3. Turn the bag over and tape the wings and folded sides to the front. Tape the ends of the wings. Punch a hole in each wing through the tape for the strings. Cut out a vent near the bottom.

b

Akela's OK   Date   Recorded by the den leader

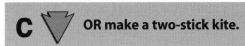

C OR make a two-stick kite.

1.

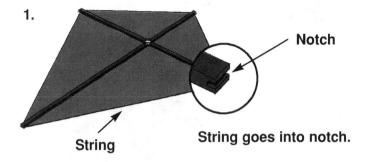

Notch

String

String goes into notch.

2.

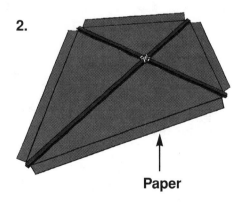

Paper

Fold paper over string and paste.

ARROW POINT
TRAIL

3.

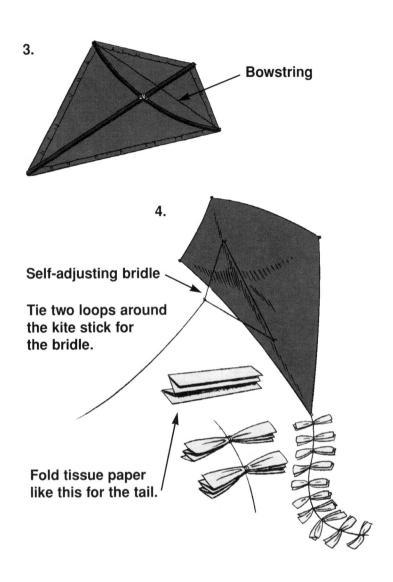

Bowstring

4.

Self-adjusting bridle

Tie two loops around the kite stick for the bridle.

Fold tissue paper like this for the tail.

C Akela's OK   Date   Recorded by the den leader

d ▽ OR make a three-stick kite.

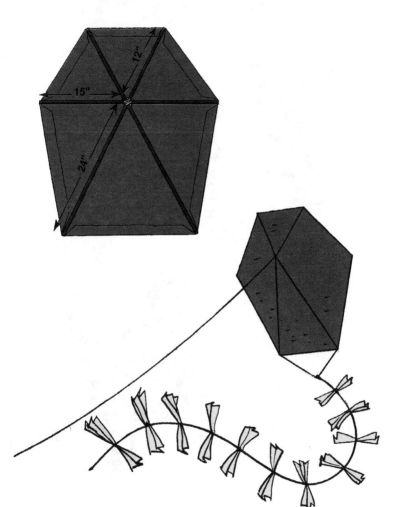

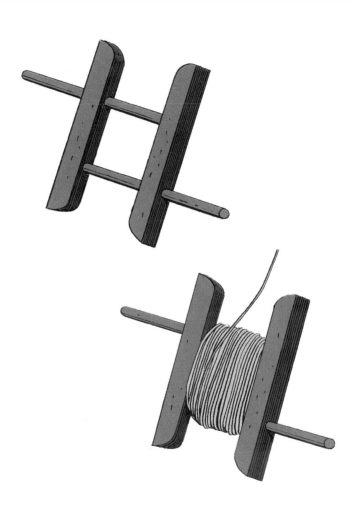

Akela's OK   Date   Recorded by the den leader

Make two holes in the propeller. Thread the rubber band through one hole and out the other. Attach it to the boat. Wind it up, and let it go!

Wind the propeller this way
to make your boat go forward.

ARROW POINT TRAIL

Akela's OK   Date   Recorded by the den leader

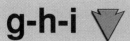
You can get credit each time you make a different model. You can count the pinewood derby car, raingutter regatta boat, or space derby rocket that you have made.

Akela's OK   Date   Recorded by the den leader

Akela's OK   Date   Recorded by the den leader

Akela's OK   Date   Recorded by the den leader

ELECTIVE Books, Books, Books

Books are magical. They are the space-ships of our minds. With them you can go anywhere.

a Visit a bookstore or go to a public library with a grown-up. Find out how to get your own library card. Name four kinds of books that interest you (for example, history, science fiction, how-to books).

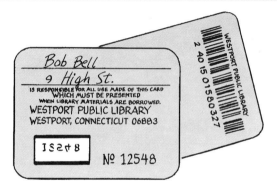

ARROW POINT TRAIL

Interesting Books

a _____
Akela's OK   Date   Recorded by the den leader

Choose a book on a subject you like and read it. With an adult, discuss what you read and what you think about it.

ARROW POINT TRAIL

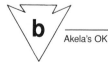 Akela's OK   Date   Recorded by the den leader

1. Hold the book on a table.

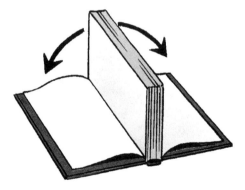

2. Let go of one cover and then the other. Put the covers down gently. Keep the pages closed and upright. Now take a few pages at a time and lightly press them down.

3. Cut paper 3 inches bigger than the book.

4. Fold the top, bottom, and right sides.

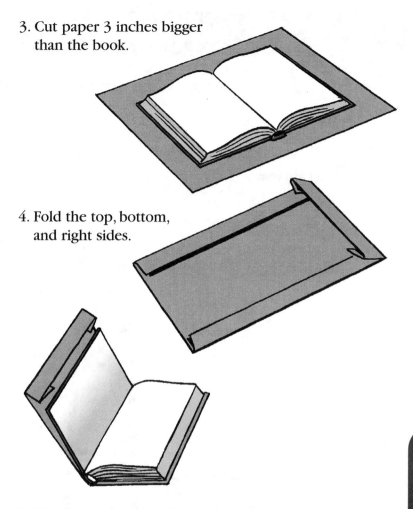

5. Slip the book cover into the right-side fold. Make a fold for the front cover. Open the book and slip the front cover into the fold.

C

Akela's OK   Date   Recorded by the den leader

Foot Power

Foot Power is a balancing act. Can you walk when your feet are off the ground? It's not as hard as it looks!

 a Learn to walk on a pair of stilts.

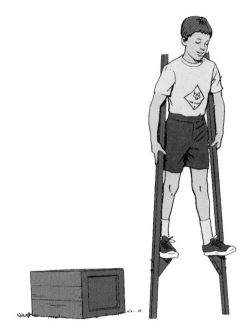

Stand on something to get started.

ARROW POINT TRAIL

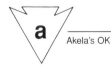

a

_____   _____

Akela's OK   Date   Recorded by the den leader

b ▼ Make a pair of "puddle jumpers" and walk with them.

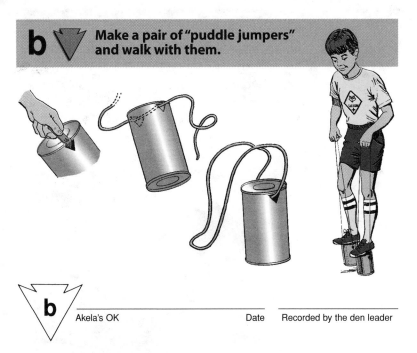

▼ b _____
Akela's OK   Date   Recorded by the den leader

c ▼ Make a pair of "foot racers" and use them with a friend.

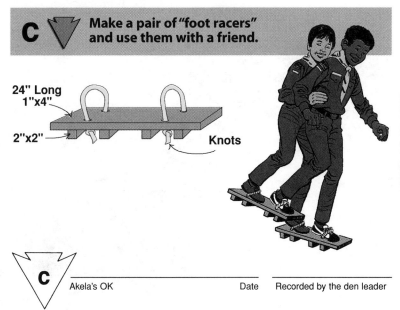

24" Long
1"x4"

2"x2"   Knots

▼ c _____
Akela's OK   Date   Recorded by the den leader

Foot Power   141

Machine Power

Learn about machines. A stick can be used as a lever. A log can be used as a wheel or a roller. Talk to workers who use levers and wheels every day.

a ▽ **Name ten kinds of trucks, construction machinery, or farm machinery.**

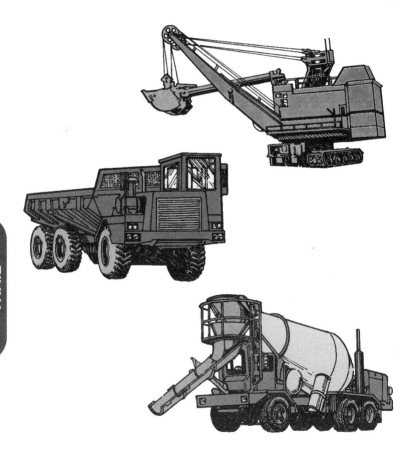

NOTE for Akela: Encourage your Cub Scout to find pictures of machinery in newspapers and magazines. He can cut them out and paste them on these pages.

a

Akela's OK   Date   Recorded by the den leader

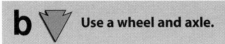

b ▽ Use a wheel and axle.

Any cart has wheels and axles.

Most of the load is on the axle.
You can move it on the wheel.

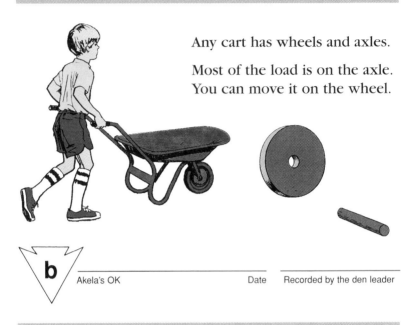

b ▽

Akela's OK

Date   Recorded by the den leader

C ▽ Use a pulley.

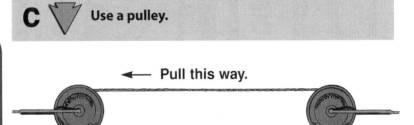

← **Pull this way.**

Line goes that way. →

Find some pulleys where you live.

C ▽

Akela's OK

Date   Recorded by the den leader

ARROW POINT
TRAIL

Arrow Point Trail • Elective 8

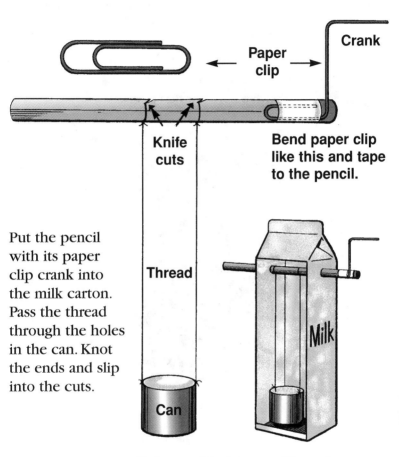

Put the pencil with its paper clip crank into the milk carton. Pass the thread through the holes in the can. Knot the ends and slip into the cuts.

Crank

Paper clip

Knife cuts

Bend paper clip like this and tape to the pencil.

Thread

Milk

Can

Cut one side from a milk carton. Punch holes for the pencil.

ARROW POINT TRAIL

d / Akela's OK   Date   Recorded by the den leader

ELECTIVE 9

Let's Have a Party

Parties are more fun when you've made a gift yourself and helped plan and put on the party.

 a Help with a home or den party.

Help decorate the room.

Help plan and play games.

Help serve refreshments.

Help clean up afterward.

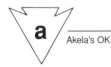

Akela's OK	Date	Recorded by the den leader

ARROW POINT TRAIL

b-c Make a gift or toy like one of these and give it to someone.

For a beanbag, use scrap cloth or an old pocket. Fill it with dried beans. Fold in the top and sew it shut.

A tin-can pencil holder can be covered with string or paper that is glued to the can.

NOTE for Akela: This gift can be given to a friend, a parent, or anyone in a hospital or retirement home. Elective credit may be given for each gift made.

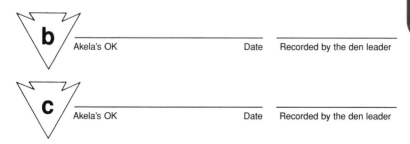

b
_____ _____ _____
Akela's OK   Date   Recorded by the den leader

c
_____ _____ _____
Akela's OK   Date   Recorded by the den leader

ARROW POINT TRAIL

Native American Lore

The first Americans were called Indians because Columbus thought he was near India when he got here. The more you know about these Native Americans, the more you will know about America.

a  Read a book or tell a story about Native Americans, past or present.

Pueblo

ARROW POINT TRAIL

I read or told a story about _____

_____

_____

_____

Akela's OK   Date   Recorded by the den leader

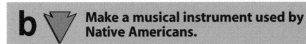

Chamois or vinyl

Cloth

Cotton

Stick

String

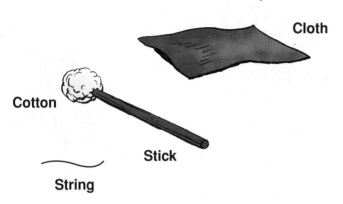

A big can or something round and hollow

b	Akela's OK	Date	Recorded by the den leader

C ▽ Make traditional clothing.

Woodland vest

Plains breechcloth

Northwest Coast hat

Pueblo belt

ARROW POINT
TRAIL

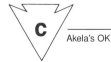

C _____
Akela's OK   Date   Recorded by the den leader

d ▽ **Make a traditional tool.**

**Plains parfleche
(bag or case)**

Plains dog travois

Piman carrying basket

Plateau snowshoe

ARROW POINT
TRAIL

 **d**

_____

Akela's OK   Date   Recorded by the den leader

Native American Lore

151

Florida stilt house

California tepee-shaped dwelling

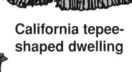

Northwest Coast plank house

Southwestern wickiup

Akela's OK   Date   Recorded by the den leader

Big voice

Bear alive

Bear dead

Bad

Top man

Camp

Brothers

Make peace

Council

Talk

Wise man

Hunt

ARROW POINT TRAIL

Morning **Noon** **Evening** **Directions**

Man **Woman** **Boy** **Man on horse**

Tepee **Hear** **Spirit** **Birds**

Eat **Deer** **Beaver** **Horses**

River	**Lake**	**Three days**	**Three nights**	**Hungry**
Fear	**Look**	**Campfire**	**Food**	
Stormy	**Clear**	**Rain**	**Cold, snow**	

Akela's OK   Date   Recorded by the den leader

Native American Lore

ELECTIVE 11 Sing-Along

Learn to sing lots of songs. There are glad songs and sad songs, and some are proud, like "The Star-Spangled Banner."

a **Learn and sing the first and last verses of "America."**

America

My country, 'tis of thee,
Sweet land of liberty,
Of thee I sing.
Land where my fathers died!
Land of the Pilgrims' pride!
From ev'ry mountainside,
Let freedom ring!

Our fathers' God, to Thee,
Author of liberty,
To Thee we sing.
Long may our land be bright
With freedom's holy light;
Protect us by Thy might,
Great God, our King!

ARROW POINT TRAIL

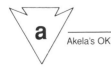

a

Akela's OK   Date   Recorded by the den leader

b Learn and sing the first verse of our national anthem.

The Star-Spangled Banner

Oh, say can you see
   by the dawn's early light
What so proudly we hailed
   at the twilight's last gleaming?
Whose broad stripes and bright stars
   through the perilous fight,
O'er the ramparts we watched
   were so gallantly streaming?
And the rocket's red glare,
   the bombs bursting in air,
Gave proof through the night
   that our flag was still there.
Oh, say does that star-spangled
   banner yet wave
O'er the land of the free
   and the home of the brave?

b

_____   _____
Akela's OK   Date   Recorded by the den leader

You can find other songs in the *Cub Scout Songbook.*

Good Night, Cub Scouts

(Tune: "Good Night, Ladies")

Good night, Cub Scouts.
Good night, Cub Scouts.
Good night, Cub Scouts,
We're going to leave you now.

Merrily we Cub along, Cub along, Cub along.
Merrily we Cub along up the Cub Scout trail.

Sweet dreams, Cub Scouts.
Sweet dreams, Cub Scouts.
Sweet dreams, Cub Scouts,
We're going to leave you now.

I Have a Dog

(Tune: "Reuben, Reuben, I've Been Thinking")

I have a dog, his name is Fido.
I have raised him from a pup.
He can stand upon his hind legs
If you hold his front legs up!

Train Song

(Tune: "Yankee Doodle")

I met an engine on a hill
All hot and broken-hearted,
And this is what he said to me
As up the hill he started.

(Slowly)

I think I can, I think I can,
At any rate, I'll try.
I think I can, I think I can,
At any rate, I'll try.

He reached the top, and looking back
To where he stood and doubted,
He started on the downward track
And this is what he shouted:

(Faster)

I knew I could, I knew I could,
I never should have doubted.
I knew I could, I knew I could,
I never should have doubted!

ARROW POINT TRAIL

C /‾‾‾‾‾‾‾‾‾‾‾‾‾‾‾‾‾‾‾‾‾‾‾‾‾‾‾‾‾   ‾‾‾‾‾‾‾‾‾‾‾‾‾‾‾‾‾‾‾‾‾
     Akela's OK   Date   Recorded by the den leader

d Learn the words and sing the first verse of three other songs, hymns, or prayers. On a piece of paper, write the verse of one of the songs you learned.

d Akela's OK _____   Date _____   Recorded by the den leader

 e Learn and sing a song that would be sung as a grace before meals. Write the words on a piece of paper.

e Akela's OK _____   Date _____   Recorded by the den leader

Arrow Point Trail • Elective 11

Sing-Along

161

ELECTIVE 12

Be an Artist

You can't tell if you can draw a picture until you try. Someday, you could become an artist or a draftsman.

a Make a freehand sketch.

Draw anything you like here or on a piece of paper.

a Akela's OK _____ Date _____ Recorded by the den leader _____

ARROW POINT TRAIL

b ▽ **Tell a story in three steps by drawing three cartoons.**

Akela's OK   Date   Recorded by the den leader

Be an Artist   163

C Mix yellow and blue paints to make green, yellow and red to make orange, and red and blue to make violet.

Color Wheel

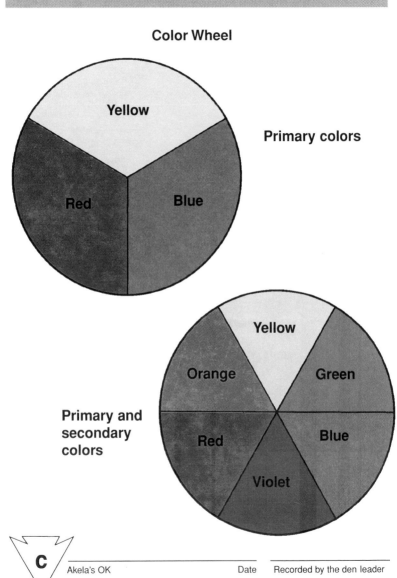

Primary colors

Primary and secondary colors

C

Akela's OK   Date   Recorded by the den leader

Help draw, paint, or crayon some scenery for a skit, play, or puppet show.

Use a large sheet of paper or cardboard.

City

Country

 Akela's OK   Date   Recorded by the den leader

ARROW POINT TRAIL

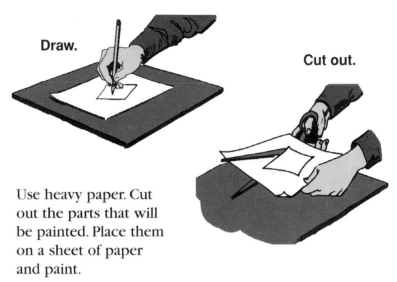

e ▽ Make a stencil pattern.

Draw.

Cut out.

Use heavy paper. Cut out the parts that will be painted. Place them on a sheet of paper and paint.

Paint.

e

_____ Akela's OK

Date   Recorded by the den leader

f Make a poster for a Cub Scout project or a pack meeting.

f _____
Akela's OK   Date   Recorded by the den leader

ELECTIVE 13 — Birds

Some birds are summer visitors. Others pass through in the spring and fall, while still others live in the same area all year. They all need homes and food.

This elective is also part of the World Conservation Award. (See page 216.)

a Make a list of all the birds you saw in a week and tell where you saw them (field, forest, marsh, yard, or park).

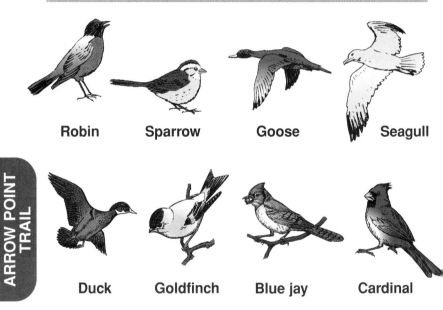

Robin Sparrow Goose Seagull

Duck Goldfinch Blue jay Cardinal

ARROW POINT TRAIL

a _____ _____
Akela's OK   Date   Recorded by the den leader

 **Put out nesting material (short pieces of yarn and string) for birds and tell which birds might use it.**

Akela's OK

Date   Recorded by the den leader

 **Read a book about birds.**

I read _____

Akela's OK

Date   Recorded by the den leader

 **Point out ten different kinds of birds (five may be from pictures).**

Akela's OK

Date   Recorded by the den leader

Birds

Feed wild birds and tell which birds you fed.

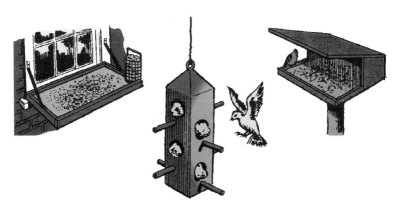

Birds like bread crumbs, cracked corn, sunflower seeds, millet, or other grains.

Make your own birdbath.

Keep the birdbath clean.

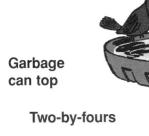

Garbage can top

Two-by-fours

Piece of broomstick

Akela's OK

Date   Recorded by the den leader

Lift the top to clean
out the birdhouse.

ARROW POINT TRAIL

Clean the birdhouse each year in the fall.

f _____

Akela's OK   Date   Recorded by the den leader

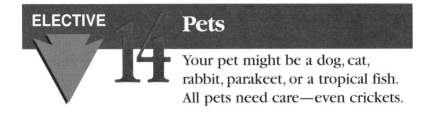

ELECTIVE 14 Pets

Your pet might be a dog, cat, rabbit, parakeet, or a tropical fish. All pets need care—even crickets.

a ▽ Take care of a pet.

ARROW POINT TRAIL

Dogs need a clean place to live. Give your dog water and dog food. Don't feed your dog small bones.

Keep your rabbit hutch clean. Feed your rabbit pellets and water.

Feed your bird birdseed, grit, and water.

Keep the cage clean.

Gerbils, hamsters, guinea pigs, white mice, and rats need prepared food, nuts, seeds, and water. Clean the cage every day.

Cats are good companions. Give them cat food, not table scraps, which contain too much fat and starch. Always keep fresh water available.

Feed fish prepared fish food. Keep the fish bowl or aquarium clean.

My pet is a _____

Its name is _____

a   _____   _____   _____
     Akela's OK   Date   Recorded by the den leader

b ▽ Know what to do when you meet a strange dog.

Do not go up to a strange dog. If a dog comes up to you

1. Stand up straight with your hands down. Let the dog sniff the back of your hand.

2. Don't make any quick moves and don't pet the dog.

3. Don't try to scare the dog away or show that you are afraid.

4. Wait until the dog leaves, then walk away quietly. Don't run.

ARROW POINT TRAIL

b _____   _____
   Akela's OK   Date   Recorded by the den leader

ARROW POINT TRAIL

I read _____

Tell what is meant by rabid. Name some animals that can have rabies. Tell what you should do if you see a dog or wild animal that is behaving strangely. Tell what you should do if you find a dead animal.

Raccoons, skunks, foxes, and bats can have rabies.

Rabid means **SICK!**

Don't go near wild animals that seem to be **TAME.**

Don't go near a dog that seems to be

CHOKING

EXCITED

AFRAID

Don't touch a dead animal.

ARROW POINT TRAIL

Tell a grown-up right away if you are bitten or scratched by any pet or wild animal, or if you find one that is sick or dead.

_____   _____

Akela's OK   Date   Recorded by the den leader

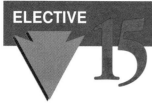

ELECTIVE   Grow Something

Growing a garden is almost like magic. You put tiny seeds into the ground, and presto, little green plants spring up.

This elective is also part of the World Conservation Award. (See page 216.)

a ▽ **Plant and raise a box garden.**

Put stones in the bottom and soil on the top. Pour water into the pipe.

| Akela's OK | Date | Recorded by the den leader |

ARROW POINT TRAIL

b ▽ **Plant and raise a flower bed.**

ARROW POINT
TRAIL

I grew _____

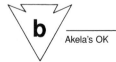

b _____   _____
Akela's OK   Date   Recorded by the den leader

Grow Something   179

C ▽ Grow a plant indoors.

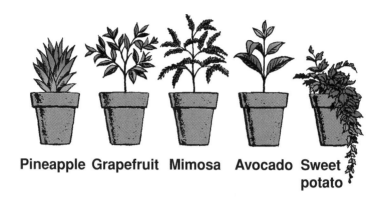

Pineapple Grapefruit Mimosa Avocado Sweet potato

Terrariums

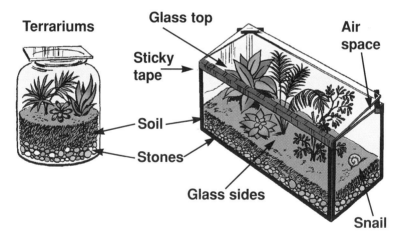

Glass top

Sticky tape

Air space

Soil

Stones

Glass sides

Snail

NOTE for Akela: Ivy, moss, and lichens will grow in a glass-covered terrarium that holds heat and moisture.

C ▽

Akela's OK   Date   Recorded by the den leader

ARROW POINT TRAIL

Do this on your own or with your family or den.

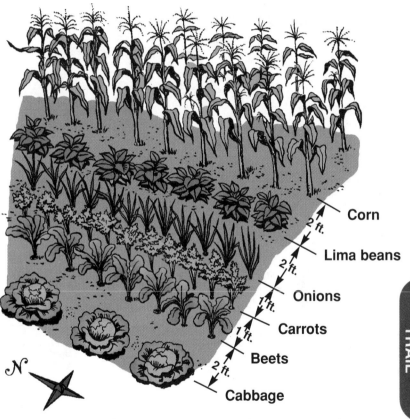

Corn

Lima beans

Onions

Carrots

Beets

Cabbage

d _____ _____
Akela's OK   Date   Recorded by the den leader

Family Alert

Would you know what to do if your home was hit by a tornado, flood, or hurricane? Here are three things you can do.

a ▽ **Talk with your family about what you will do in an emergency.**

In case of a fire we will _____

_____

_____

My job is to _____

_____

_____

NOTE to Akela: Guide your son in this project, depending upon your own home, needs, and types of emergencies in your area.

a _____   _____
    Akela's OK   Date   Recorded by the den leader

b ▽ **In case of a bad storm or flood, know where you can get safe food and water in your home. Tell how to purify water. Show one way. Know where and how to shut off water, electricity, gas, or oil.**

ARROW POINT TRAIL

I purified water by _____

_____

_____

We have emergency food and clothing in the _____

_____

NOTE for Akela: Boil water for 5 minutes. Ask a health officer for other methods.
Tell your Cub Scout where he can get safe food and water in an emergency.

b _____   _____
Akela's OK   Date   Recorded by the den leader

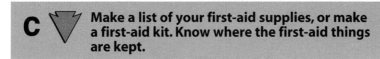

C **Make a list of your first-aid supplies, or make a first-aid kit. Know where the first-aid things are kept.**

c _____   _____
Akela's OK   Date   Recorded by the den leader

ARROW POINT TRAIL

Tie It Right

Do your shoes come untied all by themselves? Maybe the knots you tie are to blame.

 a **Learn to tie an overhand knot and a square knot.**

Overhand knot

Square knot

A square knot begins with an overhand knot and ends with another one backwards on top of the first.

_____   _____
Akela's OK   Date   Recorded by the den leader

1

2

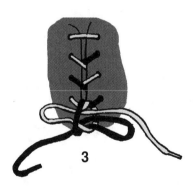

3

4

Akela's OK   Date   Recorded by the den leader

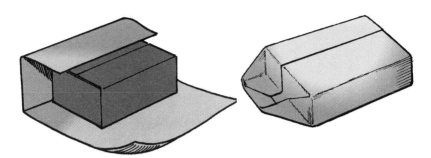

1. Put the package in the middle of the paper.

2. Fold over the long sides of the paper. Fold in the ends.

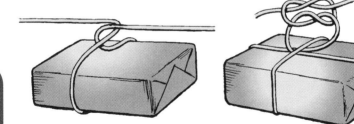

3. Take the string or ribbon once around and then cross over.

4. Flip the package over and tie with a square knot.

ARROW POINT TRAIL

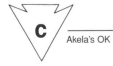

Akela's OK   Date   Recorded by the den leader

d Tie a stack of newspapers the right way.

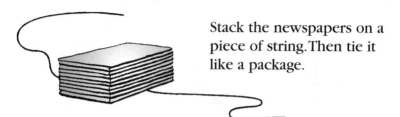

Stack the newspapers on a piece of string. Then tie it like a package.

 d

Akela's OK   Date   Recorded by the den leader

 **e** Tie two cords together with an overhand knot.

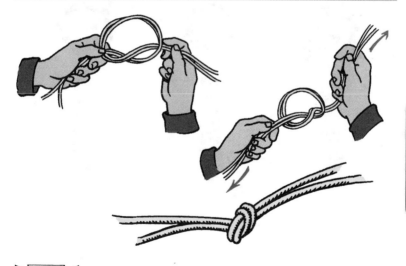

ARROW POINT TRAIL

 e

Akela's OK   Date   Recorded by the den leader

1   2   3

4   5   6

_____   _____
Akela's OK   Date   Recorded by the den leader

g ▽ **Wrap the end of a rope with tape to keep it from unwinding.**

Twisted rope

Braided rope

g

_____   _____   _____
Akela's OK   Date   Recorded by the den leader

ELECTIVE 18

Outdoor Adventure

A lot of Cub Scouting belongs outdoors with picnics, treasure hunts, and adventure trails.

a ▽ Help plan and hold a picnic with your family or den.

a ▽ _____   _____
    Akela's OK   Date   Recorded by the den leader

b ▽ With a parent, help plan and run a family or den outing.

b ▽ _____   _____
    Akela's OK   Date   Recorded by the den leader

ARROW POINT TRAIL

190   Arrow Point Trail • Elective 18

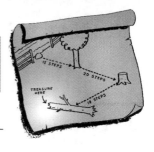

c ▽ Help plan and lay out a treasure hunt something like this.

I hid my treasure _____

_____

_____

_____ _____
Akela's OK   Date   Recorded by the den leader

d ▽ Help plan and lay out an obstacle race. Use this idea or make up your own.

- Jump across an imaginary river.
- Crawl through a cardboard tunnel.
- Jump up and ring a bell.
- Toss a ball into a can.
- Do one forward roll.
- Walk like an elephant for five steps.

This is what I did: _____

_____

_____

_____ _____
Akela's OK   Date   Recorded by the den leader

In a park or playground, set up five games scattered around the park. Here are five examples:

1
Guess how many beans are in a jar.

2
List as many insects as you can find in 2 minutes.

3
Fold the U.S. flag and read the OUTDOOR CODE:
As an American,
I will do my best to—
Be clean in my outdoor manners,
Be careful with fire,
Be considerate in the outdoors, and
Be conservation minded.

4
Tie your shoes with your eyes shut.

5
Look for colors; listen for sounds.

ARROW POINT TRAIL

▽ **e**

_____ _____ _____
Akela's OK   Date   Recorded by the den leader

f Take part in two summertime pack events with your den.

 f _____   _____
Akela's OK   Date   Recorded by the den leader

 **g** Point out poisonous plants. Tell what to do if you accidentally touch one of them.

Poison ivy   **Poison sumac**   **Poison oak**

If you touch these plants, wash with soap and water. You can also buy special outdoor skin cleansers at the store that work better than soap and water.

g _____   _____
Akela's OK   Date   Recorded by the den leader

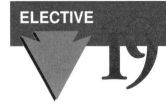

ELECTIVE 19

Fishing

In fishing, boys and grown-ups are equal. The fish does not know how old the person is at the other end of the line.

This elective is also part of the World Conservation Award. (See page 216.)

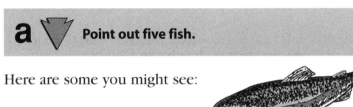

a Point out five fish.

Here are some you might see:

Rainbow trout

Bluegill

Perch

Largemouth bass

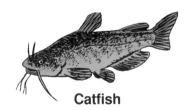

Catfish

ARROW POINT TRAIL

a _____

Akela's OK   Date   Recorded by the den leader

b Rig a pole with the right kind of line and hook. Attach a bobber and sinker, if you need them. Then go fishing.

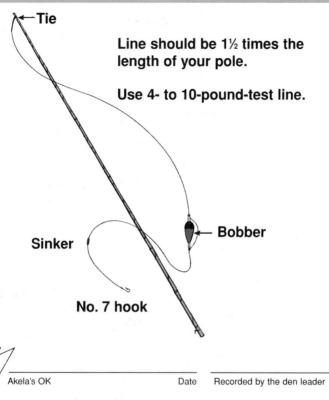

←Tie

Line should be 1½ times the length of your pole.

Use 4- to 10-pound-test line.

Bobber

Sinker

No. 7 hook

b

_____   _____   _____
Akela's OK   Date   Recorded by the den leader

c Fish with members of your family or a grown-up. Bait your hook and catch a fish.

I caught a _____

c

_____   _____   _____
Akela's OK   Date   Recorded by the den leader

d ▽ **Know the rules of safe fishing.**

Don't fish here. The bank could cave in.

Watch out for holes and drop-offs.

Be careful of slippery logs and rocks.

That fishhook can catch more than fish. Be careful around other people.

d ▽ _____

Akela's OK   Date   Recorded by the den leader

e ▽ **Tell about some of the fishing laws where you live.**

e ▽ _____

Akela's OK   Date   Recorded by the den leader

Show how to use a rod and reel.

1. Hold the line with your finger.

2. Cast the rod forward; let up on the line with your finger. When the bait or lure is where you want it, stop the reel by pressing on its edge with a finger.

3. Be sure you have plenty of room.

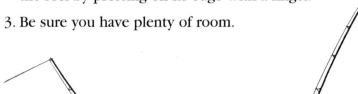

4. Reel in slowly. If a fish grabs the bait (a "strike"), play the fish and land it.

5. If you don't get a strike, reel in the line and cast again.

NOTE for Akela: Cub Scouts should have proper instruction in using rods and reels. Point out safety measures. Adults should go fishing with them.

ARROW POINT TRAIL

f _____   _____
    Akela's OK   Date   Recorded by the den leader

Sports

Before beginning this elective, discuss sportsmanship* with Akela or another adult.

a **Play a game of tennis, table tennis, or badminton.**

NOTE for Akela: Find someone who knows the game to help you. Also see the Cub Scout Sports booklets *Badminton, Tennis,* and *Table Tennis.*

a

_____ _____
Akela's OK   Date   Recorded by the den leader

See the inside front cover of any Cub Scout Sports booklet.

b ▽ **Know boating safety rules.**

1. Go boating only
   with a grown-up.

2. Don't overload
   the boat. Wear
   a personal
   flotation device.

3. Stay with the boat
   even if it leaks. It will
   keep you afloat.

4. When you see lightning or a
   storm coming, head for shore.

b

_____   _____
Akela's OK   Date   Recorded by the den leader

ARROW POINT
TRAIL

Know archery safety rules. Know how to shoot properly. Put four of six arrows into a 1.2-meter target that is fifteen steps away from you.

Archery Safety Rules

- Shoot only when a grown-up is with you.

- When handling a bow with an arrow in it (when the arrow is *nocked*), always point the arrow in a safe direction.

- Nock the arrow only when told.

- Nock the arrow only when on the firing line.

- Always point the arrow down-range toward the target.

- When not shooting, always point the arrow downward.

- Never shoot straight up in the air.

- Never shoot toward anything other than the target.

- Never shoot a bow without an arrow. You could break the bow.

NOTE for Akela: Find an archer who can help you. Also see the Cub Scout Sports booklet *Archery*.

Akela's OK   Date   Recorded by the den leader

Arrow Point Trail • Elective 20

d Understand the safety and courtesy code for skiing. Show walking and the kick turn. Do climbing with a side step or herringbone. Show the snowplow or stem turn, and how to get up from a fall.

Skier's Safety and Courtesy Code

• Good skiers always ski under control. This means you must be able to turn and stop at will so that you can avoid running into trees and other skiers.

• Make sure your ski binding holds your foot firmly to your ski and that your release works properly.

• Ski properly clothed and only when weather and conditions permit.

• Ski in an area that matches your abilities.

• Respect the rights of other skiers.

• Keep yourself physically fit.

• When skiing downhill and overtaking another skier, stay clear of the other person. Prevent collisions.

• When you and another skier are headed toward each other always stay to the right.

• Do not stop in the middle of a trail. If you fall or must stop, get off to the side of the trail. If your fall left a hole, or sitzmark, fill it with loose snow.

ARROW POINT TRAIL

- When entering a trail from the side, look up the trail to make sure no skier is coming down. The same holds true when you stop. Check up the slope before you continue to ski down the mountain.

- Never walk on ski trails without skis on your feet.

- Your skis should be equipped with a safety strap or spring-type prongs that grab into the snow when released.

- Read and obey all traffic signs on the ski slopes.

- When using a ski lift, do not cut into the line. Wait your turn.

NOTE for Akela: Find a skier who can help you. Also see the Cub Scout Sports booklet *Skiing*.

d

Akela's OK   Date   Recorded by the den leader

Know the safety rules for ice skating. Skate, without falling, as far as you can walk in fifty steps. Come to a stop. Turn from forward to backward.

Ice-Skating Safety Rules

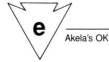

Wear warm clothes!

- Always use sharp skates.

- Skate only on safe ice in places where skating is supervised.

- Never skate alone.

- Never skate or walk on thin ice.

- Never throw anything onto the ice.

- Never push or grab another skater.

NOTE for Akela: Find a skater who can help you. Also see the Cub Scout Sports booklet *Skating*.

ARROW POINT TRAIL

_____ _____ _____
Akela's OK   Date   Recorded by the den leader

f In roller skating, know the safety rules. From a standing start, skate forward as far as you can walk in fifty steps. Come to a stop within ten walking steps. Skate around a corner one way without coasting. Then do the same coming back. Turn from forward to backward.

Indoor Skating Rules

- Fast skating is not allowed.

- When entering the skating floor, give the right-of-way to other skaters.

- In leaving, move slowly to your right. Don't cut across the path of other skaters.

- Do not push or play games that bother other skaters.

- Skate only in the direction of the skating traffic.

NOTE for Akela: Find a skater who can help you. Also see the Cub Scout Sports booklet *Skating*.

ARROW POINT TRAIL

Outdoor Skating Rules

- On sidewalks, give walkers the right-of-way.

- Don't race out of driveways or alleys.

- Avoid skating on rough pavement.

- Don't skate on other people's property without permission.

- Stop and look both ways before you cross a street.

- Obey traffic laws, signs, and signals.

- Don't skate in the street in traffic.

- Avoid uncontrolled coasting down hills.

- Don't hitch onto bicycles, cars, or trucks.

- Don't skate at night.

- Check your equipment before skating. Be sure all fittings are tight.

- Wear a helmet, gloves, wrist guards, and pads.

ARROW POINT TRAIL

NOTE for Akela: ANSI- or Snell-approved helmet; padded gloves; wrist supports; and elbow, knee, and hip pads should be worn for skating.

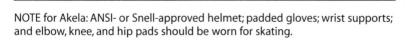

Akela's OK   Date   Recorded by the den leader

g  Go bowling.

Be a Good Sport

- Wear bowling shoes.

- Choose one bowling ball and use it.

- Bowl when it's your turn.

- Stay in your approach lane.

- Step back off the approach lane when you have finished your delivery. This lets bowlers in other lanes bowl without distraction.

- Pick up the ball with both hands, one on either side of the ball, to avoid pinched fingers and hands.

- Keep the ball on the ball return where it won't roll off and hurt someone.

- Check shoelaces and be sure they are tied.

- Return the bowling ball to the storage rack and rental shoes to the counter.

NOTE for Akela: See the Cub Scout Sports booklet *Bowling*.

ARROW POINT TRAIL

g

_____   _____
Akela's OK   Date   Recorded by the den leader

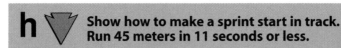
Show how to make a sprint start in track. Run 45 meters in 11 seconds or less.

(The runs in the Olympic Games are measured in meters. A meter is equal to 39.37 inches.)

Do a standing long jump of at least 1.2 meters.

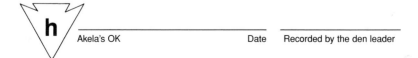
Akela's OK   Date   Recorded by the den leader

ARROW POINT TRAIL

NOTE for Akela: Find someone who knows the game to help you.

Akela's OK   Date   Recorded by the den leader

 **Show how to dribble and kick a soccer ball. Take part in a game.**

NOTE for Akela: See the Cub Scout Sports booklet *Soccer*.

Akela's OK   Date   Recorded by the den leader

k  **Play a game of baseball or softball.**

NOTE for Akela: See the Cub Scout Sports booklets *Softball* and *Baseball*.

 k _____ _____
Akela's OK   Date   Recorded by the den leader

l  **Show how to shoot, pass, and dribble a basketball. Take part in a game.**

NOTE for Akela: See the Cub Scout Sports booklet *Basketball*.

l _____ _____
Akela's OK   Date   Recorded by the den leader

ARROW POINT TRAIL

ELECTIVE

Computers

Computers can make jobs or
learning new things easier, and
computer games can be fun.

a **Visit a place where computers are used.
Find out what they do.**

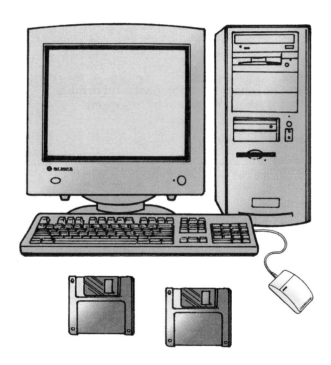

ARROW POINT
TRAIL

Akela's OK   Date   Recorded by the den leader

b Explain what a computer program does. Use a program to write a report for school, to write a letter, or for something else.

 **b**

Akela's OK _____ Date _____ Recorded by the den leader

 c Tell what a computer mouse is. Describe how a CD-ROM is used.

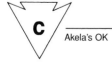 **c**

Akela's OK _____ Date _____ Recorded by the den leader

Being able to say what you mean is very important.

a Say "hello" in a language other than English.

FRENCH *allô*

GERMAN *hallo*

HEBREW *shalom*

ITALIAN *buon gior*

SPANISH *hola*

SWAHILI *jambo*

SWEDISH *hej*

AROW POINT TRAIL

 a

_____ Akela's OK

Date   Recorded by the den leader

	FRENCH	GERMAN	ITALIAN	SPANISH
1	un	eins	uno	uno
2	deux	zwei	due	dos
3	trois	drei	tre	tres
4	quatre	vier	quattro	cuatro
5	cinq	fünf	cinque	cinco
6	six	sechs	sei	seis
7	sept	sieben	sette	siete
8	huit	acht	otto	ocho
9	neuf	neun	nove	nueve
10	dix	zehn	dieci	diez

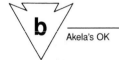

Akela's OK   Date   Recorded by the den leader

ARROW POINT TRAIL

Get story ideas from *Boys' Life* and other magazines.

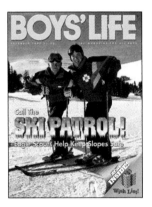

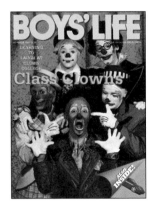

C ▽ _____
Akela's OK

Date   Recorded by the den leader

d Tell how to get to a nearby fire station or police station from your home, your den meeting, and school. Use directions and street names.

d
Akela's OK   Date   Recorded by the den leader

e Invite a boy to join Cub Scouting or help a new Cub Scout through the Bobcat trail.

I invited _____

e
Akela's OK   Date   Recorded by the den leader

Cub Scout World Conservation Award

The World Conservation Award is an international award you can earn by doing the following things:

Wolf Cub Scouts

_____ Complete Achievement 7.

_____ Complete all Arrow Points in two of the following three electives:

    _____ 13. Birds

    _____ 15. Grow Something

    _____ 19. Fishing

_____ Participate in a den or pack conservation project in addition to the above.

After you have done all of these things, ask your den leader to order your award.

Approved _____
Akela

ARROW POINT TRAIL

Cub Scout Sports and Academics

You can have fun and learn new skills when you take part in the Cub Scout Sports and Academics program. You can also earn a belt loop just for learning about a sport or academic subject and participating in it. You can take part at home, in your den or pack, or in activities in your community. There are twenty-nine Sports and Academics subjects for you to choose from.

 Archery

 Art

 Badminton

 Baseball

 Basketball

 Bicycling

 Bowling

 Citizenship

 Communicating

 Computers

 Fishing

ARROW POINT TRAIL

Geography

 Golf

 Gymnastics

 Heritages

 Marbles

 Mathematics

 Music

 Physical Fitness

 Science

 Skating

 Skiing

 Soccer

 Softball

 Swimming

 Table Tennis

 Tennis

 Ultimate

 Volleyball

Sports and Academics

Each Sports and Academics subject has a special book just for you to use to learn all about it. If you decide to continue your participation in a Sports or Academics subject over a period of time, you can earn a Cub Scout Sports or Academics pin. You can earn 1 point for every 30 minutes of activity. When you earn 60 points in a 90-day period, you have earned a Sports pin. Most Academics pins are earned in the same way, but some of them have different requirements, so check the individual book before you start.

You can even earn a letter in Cub Scout Sports and Academics like the ones shown here. You must earn a belt loop and a pin and also get a grown-up involved in earning a pin.

Ask your den leader to tell you more about Cub Scout Sports and Academics.

Get Set for Bear

When you have finished the second grade (or are 9 years old), you can start working on the achievements and electives in the *Bear Cub Scout Book.*

In the *Bear Book* you can choose twelve out of twenty-four achievements to earn your Bear badge. You will have a lot of fun learning about God, your country, your family, and yourself.

You will also have twenty-four new, fun electives to work on to earn Arrow Points.

ARROW POINT
TRAIL

BEAR

Do your best as a Wolf Cub Scout, then join the fun as you work with your parents, your den leader, your Cub Scout friends, and Baloo on the Bear Cub Scout trail.

Trail Summary

Your name _____

 BOBCAT TRAIL

 WOLF TRAIL

 ARROW POINT TRAIL

NOTE for Akela: Pages 221–26 may be reproduced when more than one boy is using the book.

Bobcat Trail

Fill in eight tracks to earn the Bobcat badge.

The Cub Scout Promise

The Law of the Pack

The Meaning of Webelos

The Cub Scout Sign

The Cub Scout Handshake

The Cub Scout Motto

The Cub Scout Salute

Exercises in *How to Protect Your Children from Child Abuse*

Wolf Trail

Fill in the Wolf tracks to show the Wolf achievements you have completed.

Achievements

1. Feats of Skill ⓐ ⓑ ⓒ ⓓ ⓔ │ ⓕ ⓖ ⓗ ⓘ ⓙ ⓚ

   Do ALL of these   and   Do ONE of these

2. Your Flag ⓐ ⓑ ⓒ ⓓ ⓔ

3. Keep Your Body Healthy ⓐ ⓑ ⓒ

4. Know Your Home and Community ⓐ ⓑ ⓒ ⓓ ⓔ

5. Tools for Fixing and Building ⓐ ⓑ ⓒ ⓓ ⓔ

6. Start a Collection ⓐ ⓑ

7. Your Living World   (a) (b) (c) (d) (e)

8. Cooking and Eating   (a) (b) (c) (d) (e)

9. Be Safe at Home and on the Street   (a) (b) (c) (d)

10. Family Fun **(Do TWO)**   (a) (b) (c) (d) (e)

11. Duty to God   (a) (b) (c)

12. Making Choices **(Do FOUR)**   (a) (b) (c) (d) (e) (f) (g) (h) (i)

Arrow Point Trail

Fill in ten arrowheads to earn a Gold Arrow Point.

Fill in ten more arrowheads to earn EACH Silver Arrow Point.

Electives

1. It's a Secret (page 104) — a b c d

2. Be an Actor (page 112) — a b c d e

3. Make It Yourself (page 118) — a b c d e

4. Play a Game (page 122) — a b c d e

5. Spare-Time Fun (page 126) — a b c d e f g h i

6. Books, Books, Books (page 136) — a b c

7. Foot Power (page 140) — a b c

8. Machine Power (page 142) — a b c d

9. Let's Have a Party (page 146) — a b c

10. Native American Lore (page 148) — a b c d e f

Notes

Notes

Notes

Notes

My Cub Scout Den

My den leader _____

_____

My assistant den leader _____

Den members _____

_____

_____

_____

_____

_____

_____

_____

_____

_____

_____